Fish the Flats

with

Tampa Bay Fishing Guide
Capt. Fred Everson

by

Capt. Fred Everson

i

Fish the Flats

Note for Librarians: a cataloguing record for this book that includes Dewey Decimal
Classification and US Library of Congress numbers is available from the Library and Archives
of Canada. The complete cataloguing record can be obtained from their online database at:
www.collectionscanada.ca/amicus/index-e.html
ISBN 1-4120-5182-7

TRAFFORD

Offices in Canada, USA, Ireland and UK
This book was published *on-demand* in cooperation with Trafford Publishing. On-demand
publishing is a unique process and service of making a book available for retail sale to the
public taking advantage of on-demand manufacturing and Internet marketing. On-demand
publishing includes promotions, retail sales, manufacturing, order fulfilment, accounting and
collecting royalties on behalf of the author.

Book sales for North America and international:
Trafford Publishing, 6E–2333 Government St.,
Victoria, BC v8t 4p4 CANADA
phone 250 383 6864 (toll-free 1 888 232 4444)
fax 250 383 6804; email to orders@trafford.com
Book sales in Europe:
Trafford Publishing (uk) Ltd., Enterprise House, Wistaston Road Business Centre,
Wistaston Road, Crewe, Cheshire cw2 7rp UNITED KINGDOM
phone 01270 251 396 (local rate 0845 230 9601)
facsimile 01270 254 983; orders.uk@trafford.com
Order online at:
trafford.com/05-0077

10 9 8 7 6 5 4 3 2

DEDICATION

I owe my outdoor living to these men; my uncles (in uniform) and my grandfather (natty dresser with the fedora). The picture was taken in January of 1945, six years before I was born. They were taking time off the water for the Second World War. But when it was over, they went back to fishing and crabbing and spearing eels on the Raritan Bay in Union Beach, New Jersey. I was baiting killie traps and dip netting blue crabs with them long before I learned my ABC's, and for that I am truly grateful. They are all gone now, but this book couldn't have been written without them, or my grandmother, who cooked what we caught and cleaned up after us all.

Fish the Flats

Capt. Fred comes by his fishing addiction honestly. He's been at it for more than 50 years, and he's still a flashy dresser.

iv

Fish the Flats

Table of Contents

The Salt Water Flats Environment

I suppose a definition of a "flat" as it relates to fishing should be the first order of business. It is not a scientific term, but most who fish in this unique environment will tell you a flat is simply a stretch of shallow water with a relatively level bottom. That description will work.

What comes as a surprise to many newcomers to flats fishing is to see other fishermen trying to catch fish in water that's little more than ankle deep. From a northern perspective where lake trout are caught in 90 feet of cold water, or offshore, where pelagics are reeled up from the ocean deep, it's seems odd to find big fish in such shallow water. But here they are, and some-

1

Fish the Flats

times the fish are very big. Tarpon and sharks weighing hundreds of pounds hunt the flats, and so do cobia.

The next surprise for the freshwater angler is how hard most of these fish pull – even small pompano and little jack crevalles. I once had a young couple on the boat from Pennsylvania. The wife was a decent angler who could cast and re-trieve with a spinning rod – a petite little lady who told me she enjoyed catching trout and bass back home. But when she hooked a big jack cre-valle and it took off on the first run, she quickly handed the rod off to her husband.

"I don't know what that thing is, but you';re not putting it on this boat!" Yup, salt water fish pull *very* hard.

Flats are different. On some the bottom is soft mud, on others it may be hard and sandy. Some are covered with seagrass and some are bare. But the most important thing to remem-ber is that none are really flat. Wind, waves, and current create changes in depth. The high spots are bars, the channels that run slightly deeper and parallel to the shoreline and the sand bars are troughs. Places where the current cuts through the bars at the end of low tide and the beginning of the rise are swash channels. Bare, sandy depressions on a grass flat are called pot holes. Knowing what these are is important, because gamefish use them as feeding stations.

2

Fish the Flats

To be successful in flats fishing, you have to be able to "read" water.

Where I fish on Tampa Bay, the flats are bordered on the shore side by mangroves. Behind this border lies an estuary that consist of creeks, passes and bayous, which are collectively called "the backcountry." Understanding the terminology is key when you try to learn anything from a book, and hopefully the illustrations will help make the whole layout of a flat clear as a low tide in winter.

3

Fish the Flats

Introduction

Current on a flat is not as perceptible as it is in a creek or pass, nevertheless the water is moving as the tide rises or falls. For a short period between tides the current may become slack, but it must begin to move again as the water is tugged one way or the other by the combined gravitational forces of the earth, moon, and sun. The more water being moved, the stronger the current will be. Stronger currents will carry more baits than weak ones, thus most fishermen like to fish peak current flows. The strongest currents and the greatest difference between high tide and low tide occur every other week when the moon is full, or the moon is new. These are called "Spring Tides." The weaker tides associated with half moon phases are called "Neap Tides."

My personal preference for flats fishing is low tide. Less water concentrates fish, whereas at high tide they can and do spread out. Nevertheless, other very good guides like Capt. Jon Turner prefer to fish the high tides. But certain flats will produce best at different stages of the tide. For example, some flats produce best on a high, falling tide, while a different flat is best fished on a low rise. This is something you will learn from experience, and it makes a good case for keeping a fishing log. Besides tide and current, other important influences on flats fishing are time of day, season, wind, water tempera-

4

Fish the Flats

ture and cloud cover. It's difficult to keep all of that in your head, but if you put in on paper long enough, patterns will begin to emerge, and understanding those patterns are apt make your fishing experience a lot more predictable.

This gap in the mangroves is called a pass. This is a likely place to look for fish for several reasons. The opening creates a funnel for current, which in turn gouges a change in depth. Combined with the shade on the dark side, this pass makes a perfect ambush point for hungry predators. Game fish will usually position themselves in the eddies just outside of the current, waiting for baitfish to be flushed through the pass. The perfect cast here would be straight down the center line of the boat into theshadows, by the point and to the right. For the most natural presentation retrieve the bait with the current.

5

Fish the Flats

In the clear shallow water on this Tampa Bay flat an accurate cast with a long rod hooked this angler up with a redfish. Casting distance and accuracy are a must in sight fishing.

6

Fish the Flats

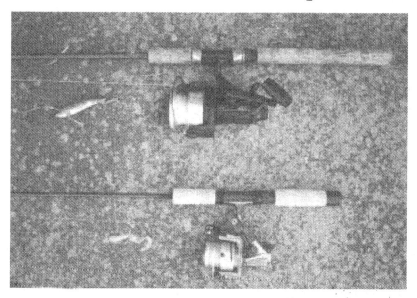

Chapter 1

Flats Tackle

You find fish in shallow water on the flats because that's where the food is — but clear, shallow water is a dangerous environment for fish up and down the food chain. See what happens when the shadow of a sea bird passes over a pod of fish on a flat. Even large snook are apt to skedaddle from the passing spectre — the memory of being preyed upon from above from fry to trophy is never forgotten.

Spooky fish in shallow water call for long casts, regardless whether rods are rigged with live bait or artificials. I prefer spinning tackle

7

Fish the Flats

for chucking light baits a long way, and if I had to pick just one rod to fish the flats with, it would be at least seven and a half feet long and rated for line somewhere between eight and 30 pound test. But there are plenty of anglers who fish the flats with baitcasting tackle, and indeed, baitcasters do some things better, so it's a matter of personal preference– as long a s the rod will toss a bait far enough to catch fish, and then have enough muscle to land the fish, it will do.

For lots of casting with artificial baits, a rod with a short handle is less tiring to fish with, and uses more of the rod during the cast than one with a long butt.

For me a spinning rod is simply less trouble, especially when casting into the wind. On other flats the casting requirement may be much shorter because of murky water, or more depth.

I build my own style flats rods on fly rod

Fish the Flats

blanks, trimming them down to 8 feet three inches, or 8 and a half feet. I don't build rods to save money but to get exactly what I want in rod performance. Still, many commercial rods are designed specifically for inshore, shallow water fishing. Daiwa's Coastal rods, and St. Croix's Tidemasters come to mind as modestly priced, good quality inshore saltwater rods.

Any rod you choose for the flats should be graphite, because of it's light weight and inherent stiffness. A lighter rod is easier to cast and less tiring to fish with; extra stiffness is important for hooksets and landing big fish without having to play them to death. Graphite is also more sensitive, which is important when fishing live bait on a slow bite. For the same reason, cork is my preferred handle material, foam handles tend to absorb vibration and decrease sensitivity.

As a fishing guide, I employ three types of rods. I use 7'9" heavy action rods for my live bait fishing around mangrove shoreline , then I have some longer, more limber rods for open water flats fishing with light line and artificials, and finally some baitcasting rigs for fishing artificials for big backcountry snook and redfish. These rods need to be stout, with extra fast tips to pry strong fish away from barnacle encrusted structure.

I rig the live bait rods with line that tests 24 pounds. I am currently using Stren Extra Strength 12 pound diameter, 24 pound break strength, but many guides prefer the microfilaments. The idea is to be able to pull rambunctious fish away from roots and pilings, and it takes tough line to do that.

A reel should be matched to the rod in terms of size. I fish several models of Daiwa and Shimano reels interchangeably, but if I had to use only one reel, it would be the Daiwa Black Gold BG20. This reel is a simple, durable workhorse that is well suited to salt water fishing. It matches up nicely with the 7'9" Daiwa Coastal Rod, or the 8' St. Croix Tidemaster. There's plenty of good tackle out there, and I'm not going to say one brand is better than another. I will tell you what I use and what I like, merely as a point of reference.

Any reel that will spool 150 yards of 10 pound test monofilament will do for open water flats fishing. But the features to look for in a reel are durability in salt water, a smooth drag, an easy bail flip, and a high speed of retrieve. Instant anti reverse is nice for fishing artifificals.

I have used some reels with coil spring bails, and I have never been able to break one of those springs. For reels that use the more traditional style spring, I keep plenty of spares on hand, and make sure that I have the tools in my tackle box to make the change. Replacing a broken bail spring requires no particular mechanical inclination. Practice the job on the

Fish the Flats

kitchen table under good light, and a broken bail spring will never interfere with a fishing trip. Carry spare springs and an appropriate screwdriver in your tackle box. If you favor revolving spool reels, you can save your concern for casting into the wind.

When I buy a new reel I put the schematic drawing into the "R" folder in my filing cabinet, after I order some spare springs from the parts list. If the reel doesn't come with a spare spool, it's a good idea to order one of those, too. Spare spools are handy for tackling up when you encounter a school of oversized redfish or big black drum, or just changing out line that get twisted or beat up.

Besides bail springs, the other thing most likely to fail on a quality reel is the drag. Playing big, powerful fish like snook, redfish, and jack crevalle with light line calls for a super smooth drag. Most drags are equipped with a series of round washers that alternate between metal and another material, such as felt, cork, or synthetic fiber. Over time these washers wear out. When that happens the drag tends to become jerky and may even stick. When a drag sticks on a big fish, the line usually parts and the battle is over, leaving the unconsolable angler to stamp his feet and forever think about what might have been. Unfortunately, it's always the big fish that find the weak leaks in your tackle. You can order

11

Fish the Flats

extra drag washers directly from the manufacturer of the reel, or from Smoothie, a company that manufactures drag washers for most of the popular reels.

That brings us to line. Again, I will tell you that I use and like Ande IGFA monofilament on my open water flats rods that I use for artificials. Many anglers have made the switch to super sensitive, multi strand, microfilament lines. I have tried most of them, but I keep going back to monofilament. Ten pound test is pretty minimal on the flats, and too light to fish around structure. but the casting and handling qualities of 8 and 10 pound test monofilament are superior for long casts on open water.

When I am fishing around the close quarters of structure, I like Stren's Extra Strength 12/24 monfilament on heavy spinning tackle. This is also the line I like to use for cobia, small tarpon, and for fishing around roots and other light structure for snook and redfish.

A stout leader is required for most flats fishing. Snook have an abrasive mouth – even small snook can routinely chafe through a 20 pound leader. Fluorocarbon is said to resist abrasion better than monofilament, but I'm not sure about that. I do use fluorocarbon in winter and spring when the water is super clear. I use 30 pound monofilament fishing line for leaders more often. Quarter pound spools store nicely in foam coolies for easy access. 24 to 30 inches is about the right length. This means I don't have to reel the knot that connects leader and line through the rod tip to cast. Casting the knot through the rod tip will eventually displace the ceramic guide ring from the frame.

Tampa Bay flats fishing requires long casts with baits and lures that probably weigh less than half an ounce. If you can't cast at least 120 feet from the boat, your catch will be sorely limited. Boats are noisy, fish spooking machines.

This means using light line on big, very rambunctious fish, which in turn calls for an exceptional knot. The improved clinch knot, or fishermen's knot is weaker than the Uni Knot — break strength of the Uni is near 100 percent. I have never tested it scientifically, but plenty of big fish have not had much success breaking uni knots -- I'm satisfied that the break strength is everything that it's supposed to be.

But strength is only one reason to use the uni knot – it is also the easiest knot to tie for the greatest number of applications. I use it to connect line and leader, to tie on hooks and lures – with and without a loop, and even to build compound fly leaders. Once learned it's very easy to tie this very strong, compact knot.

Fish the Flats

Custom Rods

There is a stigma about custom built fishing rods that comes from overly fancy rods built for guys who can afford to pay a lot for them. Then there is the other custom rod, the one that a fisherman designs from the blank up because he can't find exactly what he wants. This is the best reason to get involved with custom rods. A rod that is perfectly matched to the way you fish and what you fish for will make an immeasurable difference in the satisfaction you get from fishing.

Chapter 1

Speckled trout are a perfect example of fish that want a rod built to spec. Trout can vary a lot in size, but they are all soft-mouthed. The weight range of baits, both live and artificial, is fairly light.

My approach to building a custom rod for open water flats fishing was based on rods I used years ago for freshwater trout. For long casts with light baits, fly rod blanks make excellent extra long, light spinning rods. I use inexpensive graphite fly rod blank, as it will never throw a flyline. You can buy everything you need to build this rod for about $50, and the rod building instructions often come with the blank. It's about a 10-hour project for a novice.

From experience, I knew what size guides I wanted. I found that more small guides are more efficient than a few that are too large. For casting baits and playing fish, I like a rod that keeps the line close to the blank with a long graceful bend under the strain of a fish. I follow the manufacturer's recommendations for guide placement like I was building a fly rod, but instead I use single foot, hardloy spinning guides, ranging in size from 25 mm to 6 mm.

Another unusual feature of my flats rod is a short butt section behind the reel seat. This makes the rod easier to cast, more nimble in a boat, and less tiring to cast again and again as you are apt to do when fishing with any artifi-

Fish the Flats

cial. Casting is sweeter because everything is scaled to size. It's the difference between swinging a 20 gauge double and a 12-gauge goose gun.

When Mark Sosin was at the shop to do a show with Capt. Chet, I noticed all his rods were tied on short handles. We compared notes and both agreed on the merits of short handles.

Ten-pound test monofilament is my three season choice, but you sacrifice some casting distance. For winter fishing for redfish and trout I go to 8 pound test to be able to cast farther in the cold, gin clear water. I fish my running line tipped with at least 18 inches of 25 pound test flourocarbon leader material. This is great stuff for toothy fish: it resists abrasion well, and it is nearly invisible in the water. It is very pricey compared to monofilament, but I believe it makes a difference in the number of fish you catch when water clarity is extreme.

Fishing with a longer, more limber rod takes some getting used to. If you have been fishing with a short, stiff rod, you will have to change your casting mechanics. With softer rods, you need to develop a sense of timing so that the action of the rod does most of the work. It is similar to the principal of loading a fly rod on the back cast, except here the weight of the lure flexes the rod.

The difference between this rod and an over the counter spinning rod is that the rod action is

16

more prominent in casting. The long whippy rod is cast with a snap of the wrist. Once you get a handle on this, you will find incredible accuracy, and very long casts with minimal effort. For the artificial bait fisherman, this means covering more water, catching more fish, and enjoying the play with a rod perfectly matched to the fish and the baits you throw.

The first concern of a fisherman who is used to a short, stiff rod is hook setting. He sees a rod with a butt diameter of a pencil and a tip the thickness of a sewing needle, and wonders how he can ever drive the hook home with that? But you don't need a hard hook set on most fish, particularly on sea trout . This fish is a close relative to weakfish, so named because they have fragile lips that tear easily under the duress of rod pressure. Here the long limber rod excels. The same soft action that aids in casting minimizes the strain on the trout's soft mouth.

Set your drag right and the hook won't pull. Hook setting is over rated in flats fishing; keeping the hook in the fish's mouth is what counts, and modern chemically sharpened hooks are way superior to anything they had in the good old days of trying to rip the fish's lips off. Even hard mouthed redfish do not require jaw breaking hook sets.

I like a small reel for my open water flats rod, one that spools 140 yards of 10 pound test

17

Fish the Flats

monofilament is about right. I always start out with the spool full of line, but the first 40 yards often throws little bird's nests. Once I get through a few of those, the line seems to settle down and behave. This doesn't leave room for error with trophy snook or bull reds, but as long as there are no obstructions you've got a chance at landing very big fish with the long rod.

If there is a negative with extremely long rods, it is their tendency to find a way into the path of slammed doors and hatches, or under-foot. I have never broken one of my long rods on fish, not even big jack crevalle, but other stuff happens. It has been said that unbreakable rods fish poorly, but I wouldn't know, because I've managed to break quite a few.

Longer rods are not more fragile by virtue of extra length. But all rods are designed to bend in an arc from butt to tip. If you go beyond the range of this arc and bend a section of the rod too far, you will get a compression fracture near the tip. This usually happens by reeling a big fish too close to the rod tip or trying to hoist it out of the water. No light tackle rod should ever be used to lift heavy fish. Always leave about a rod's length of line between the rod tip and the hook when trying to land a fish, and you won't break a tip. With a longer rod it is easier to grab hold of the leader if you can keep the rod tip high in the air. This also maintains steady pressure on the

18

hook, so fish can't flop off.

There is nothing quite like catching fish on tackle that's perfectly matched to the task at hand. And if you build the rod yourself, the satisfaction of casting it well, and enjoying of the play on big fish will take your flats fishing to a new level.

Capt. Chaz Waltz of Apollo Beach has his rod in the right position as he prepares to land his fish. Always leave a rod's length of line between the rod tip and the fish and the leader will come in easy reach when the rod tip is pointed straight up.

Fish the Flats

A Case for Bait Casters

That spinning reels are easier to use than bait casting reels is unquestionable. Yet bait casters still fill a prominent niche in the world of fishing tackle, and the reason for that is bait casters simply do some things better than spinning reels do.

Plug casting comes to mind first. A bait-casting rig is much better suited to throwing a ¾ ounce plug accurately, and it's also much easier to work the plug with the inherently stiffer, shorter bait-casting rod. They don't call 'em plug rods for nothing.

The problem with bait casters is backlashes, which occur when the spool revolves faster than the line is being paid out. Reel manufacturers have made great strides using magnets and brakes to minimize the problem, but it will probably never be eliminated. I currently employ two bait casting reels , a Shimano Cardiff and an Abu Garcia Ambassador – both of them left handed – both high quality, high performance reels, and there are many, many more high quality reels from a variety of manufactures, at every level of the price spectrum.

The learning curve for mastering the bait caster is longer than that of the spinning reel, but anglers made do with it for years. Matching reel adjustments to the lure and learning to thumb the spool to prevent the dreaded backlash takes practice, but with time, casting accuracy will improve, and rod handling skills will evolve.

Besides casting accuracy, bait-casters afford better line control around the mangrove roots, pilings, and other structure. When targeting big snook in the backcountry, a bait-caster is my tool of choice. Here I can bump monofilament line up to 20-pound test without affecting casting distance or accuracy. And when a fish does strike on the shadow line, I can thumb the spool and put the rod to it, and pry the fish away from the roots. Not that you can't do this with a spinning reel spooled with superline, just that the bait-caster does it better. There is an

21

Fish the Flats

economy of motion, in cast and in retrieve that also make the bait-caster less tiring to fish with.

My other problem with bait-casting reels is that I learned to fish them left-handed. This means that I cast with the right hand and reel with the left, and it's a good problem to have. For right handers who have never laid hands on a bait casting reel, this is the way to go, because it eliminates the clumsiest step in traditional style bait-casting, that of having to switch the rod from the right hand to the left after the cast. If you are right handed, your right arm is probably strongest, and that's the hand you should want the rod in. The same thing is true for fly fishing tackle. Traditional right handed fly fishermen make the cast with the right hand and then switch the rod to the left to retrieve. Why? Because that's how the tackle was originally designed. But if you are right handed, and you have never used a bait caster or fly rod, why not set up all your reels for left handed retrieve? That way you can always keep the rod in your right hand. However, if you have learned to fish traditional style, it's probably best left alone, because left hand retrieve will never feel natural.

My fishing buddy Vic Stephens is a prime example of how crazy this right hand left hand stuff can be. He fishes spinning tackle as a left-hander should – casting with the left hand and reeling with the right. But he is primarily a bait

22

casting man, and with this tackle he fishes right handed – casting with the right hand, then switching the rod to his left and retrieving with the right. He learned to fish this way because right-handed reels predominate in bait-casting, whereas with a spinning reel you can easily switch the reel handle from left to right – an option not afforded on revolving spool reels.

As a general rule, bait-casting rods are shorter and stiffer than spinning rods. My friends Captains Bryan and Greg Watts, fish primarily with bait casting tackle, and they do it about as well as anyone can. They win more than their share of professional saltwater tournaments, and as artificial experts, it is no accident that they prefer bait-casters. Another friend, Keli Emery, one of Tampa Bay's premiere lady anglers is another bait-casting fan. She specializes in fishing live baits for big tripletail, and likes the control bait-casters afford in dragging these big, powerful fish away from range markers and buoy chains.

No doubt about it, bait-casting tackle requires more skill and effort to use than spinning tackle does. But when fishing for big, powerful fish around structure, the revolving spool reel simply affords superior control. The star drag is easily adjusted without having to let go of the reel handle, or you can merely apply thumb pressure to assist the drag in the heat of battle with

23

Fish the Flats

a much greater economy of motion than is possible with a spinning reel. Having a bait-casting rig in your arsenal and knowing how, when and where to use it will definitely elevate your fishing game.

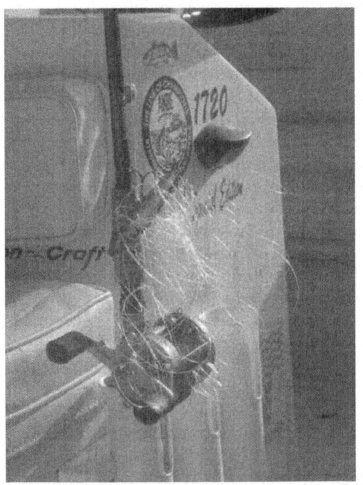

An occasional backlash will ever be a part of bait casters. Nevertheless, they still excell at plug casting. This one occurred when the hook pulled on a big snook.

24

Chapter 2

Accessories for Flats Fishing

Florida flats fishing calls for a thoughtful approach to clothing, tools, and miscellaneous other accessories, because this is more like hunting than casual fishing. What you wear is important not only because the sun can be intense on a mid day flat, but also because certain colors blend better with the surroundings. White hats and white shirts should be avoided because they reflect the most light. White may be a cool choice, but a flash of white will also alarm fish, which

25

Fish the Flats

are bound to associate that with the wings of predatory shore birds. Tan, green, light blue and other earth tones are less obtrusive and will serve better than bright and bawdy hats and shirts.

A hat serves to keep the sun off your head and out of your eyes. A wide brim hat will also protect the tips of your ears, but the protection afforded by any hat should be supplemented with a liberal dose of sunscreen. I like to apply the sunscreen at home so I can wash my hands with soap and water to keep it off my tackle and out of the live wells. Wind and sun also wrecks my lips, so there is always a Chap Stick in my tackle box.

Perhaps the most important accessory in shallow water sight fishing is a pair of polarized sunglasses. Polarized glasses cut the glare off the surface of the water, and are an absolute must. The glasses need not be expensive to be effective. Side shields help you see better when the sun is off to one side or the other. And for the over 40 set, you can even buy polarized bifocals so you don't have to switch glasses to tie knots. To keep my glasses where I can find them, I like the eyeglass holders that resemble surgical tubing. And to clean the salt spray off the lenses, I keep a paper towel moistened with window cleaner in a plastic bag in my shirt pocket. Being able to see the fish well makes the flats fishing game a lot more exciting, and productive.

Fish the Flats

Next to sunglasses, the tool I rely on most when fishing the flats is pair of fishing pliers. My pliers have spring loaded parallel jaws and a great little line cutter on the side. I carry them in a leather sheath on my belt, and to try fishing without the pliers in place is a lot like fishing naked. And cheap pliers literally won't cut it.

Two other tools I carry on the boat play an important part in catch and release fishing. A hook remover is easier on fish than needle nose pliers, and it also helps keep your hands and fingers out of hurms way. Saltwater catfish will hurt you if they break the skin with their spines. My de-hooker is long enough to stay away from shark teeth and stingray barbs, and works well with forged live bait hooks – however it will destroy light wire hooks.

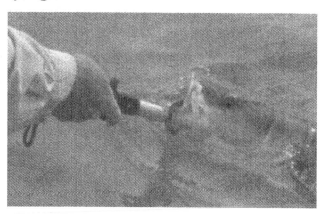

A lip-gripping tool is useful in that it precludes having to put the fish in a net. The majority of fish t I catch are going to be released,

Fish the Flats

so I don't net many.   The net's mesh scrapes slime off the scales and increases the chance of fatality.   No honor in releasing a fish if you're not going give it its best chance to survive. Snook, redfish, and trout tend to relax when picked up by placing a hand under the center of the belly.

Those fish that I intend to kill and eat, I place in an iced cooler soon as they're landed. Putting a fish in a live well all day is not the best way to keep fish that are headed for the table. Give the fish a break, and ice it right away — keeping a fish alive in confinement has to be stressful, and that can't do much to enhance flavor

Another handy accessory is a boat towel. I buy white terry cloth shop towels by the bundle, and they are great for wiping the gunk off your hands, drying off seats and general clean up, but avoid a using the towel to handle fish that will be released; it can do even more harm than a landing net.   I keep several paper towels in a dry box with my first aid kit, and all of my boat paperwork. Sunscreen and insect repellent are stored in the same box.

Managing Tackle

The best way to manage tackle is to minimize selection. I carry a spool each of 30 and 60 pound monofilament for leader material.

28

Fish the Flats

I prefer quarter pound spools because they fit into a foam coolie for which I have a plastic holder on my console. My leader material is always handy this way and easy to dispense.

I carry a few packs of #1 live bait hooks in my shirt pocket. In my tackle box is a selection of floats, and some wire leaders, barrel swivels, split rings, extra treble hooks, and a pair of split ring pliers. I also have two small screwdrivers -- phillips head, and slotted -- for working on reels.

I have tried everything in the way of tackle boxes and finally returned to the old style plastic box I started with. When it got too small to hold all of my tackle I got bigger and badder boxes when I should have been reducing inventory. Now I know. Minimize your lure selection, learn to fish a small number of lures that cover the water column, and soon you will begin to figure out what works where.

Fish the Flats

This fish is coming into the danger zone. Play fish out away from the boat. Don't reel against the drag. Maintain constant, relentless pressure and keep a good bend in the rod.

Fish the Flats

Chapter 3

Flats Boats and Boating Accessories

The first flats boat I bought was a tunnel hull with a center console and a poling platform. It was a nice boat to fish from, but the manufacturer cut a few corners. He left out stringers and a lot of the fiberglass. The 30 gallon live well was supplied by a 360 gph pump, and it was little more than a chamber of death . Even pinfish could barely survive for more than a few minutes.

Worse than that, the entire design concept of the skiff was dangerous. Once water got into the sponsons, there was no way to get it out, other than to put the boat on the trailer and unscrew

31

Fish the Flats

the brass plugs. The cockpit was supposed to be self bailing, but if two anglers stood on either side of the stern, water rushed in through the drains and cascaded into the hull through the hole in the deck that channeled wiring and controls. The point is this; all fiberglass boats are not created equal, and the reason some cost more than others *usually* has to do with quality. The first thing I would do if I was looking for a new boat would be to rap on the hull a few times with my knuckles. Not very scientific, but notwithstanding it will tell you something about hull construction. Beyond that, I would seek a boat manufacturer that had some history to back up his advertisements, and then I would like to talk to someone who owned the type of boat I was looking to buy.

There are a many hull styles to choose from. "V" hulls will give the best ride, but draw more water than tunnel hulls and flat bottom skiffs. There is no perfect choice, so I will simply tell you how I arrived at my selection. Where you fish, how shallow you want to get, and how many people you want to carry, are the most important considerations.

I knew I would be traveling the length and breadth of Tampa Bay. But I wanted a small enough skiff to pole in 10 inches of water. That rules out 20 foot bay boats. Distance made a shallow V hull a better choice for me, however there are plenty of fishermen who travel the same

32

distance in tunnel hulls and flat bottomed boats.

I opted for a 17 foot Action Craft Bay Runner because there was a dealer nearby, and I liked the hull design. I've had the boat six years now, and I am happy with the overall quality. It's quiet and solid, and the ride is good for a small boat. It carries two anglers and myself comfortably, and will carry an additional angler if it has to, but two is better than three. I can range over Tampa Bay with clients aboard, but if the wind blows more than ten knots across the beam, we are going to get wet.

The cockpit is designed so that it can be plugged to be either self bailing, or water can be channeled into the bilge. This is handy in rough seas when the waves are rolling over the bow, because you don't have to rely on the bilge pump – the water will exit through the drains in the side of the hull.

I also opted for a poling platform instead of a tower because I like to fish artificials more than I do live bait. Towers offer the advantage of being able to look for fish or for bait on plane, but forget about fly-fishing from a tower boat. The tower is basically an encumbrance for fishing with anything other than live bait – but that's only my humble opinion.

Despite a preference for fishing with lures, much of my guide fishing is done with live bait. For less skilled anglers, live bait is simply more

33

Fish the Flats

productive, so a thoughtfully designed live well system is a necessity. There is nothing complicated about this. A through hull high speed pick up, proper aeration, and a timer on the pump switch combine to keep bait alive all day. When I bought my boat, both wells were served by a single pump and switch. I installed a separate thru hull pick up, and a second pump on it's own switch, to serve the boat with two independent live-well systems. I also use cartridge pumps to facilitate changing them out when they fail – and fail they do, which is why I installed a second pump.

Dry storage on most flats boats is ever at a premium, so I employ a portable dry box to carry all the stuff that needs to be absolutely dry – camera, cell phone, wallet, first aid kit, etc.

Of Push Poles and Poling Skiffs

With the ever-increasing popularity of tower boats, I am a dinosaur among Tampa Bay fishing guides. But my boat is well suited to the traditional method of sight fishing, which involves poling the flats or poling mangrove shoreline. Progress is slow and stealthy, but it is not as productive in terms of sighting fish as running around on plane with a tower boat, however it is way less intrusive. You may cover a lot more water with a tower, and catch more fish

Fish the Flats

with live bait, but there is still much to be said for poling. Poling a skiff is the quietest way to move around in shallow water besides wading, and if you would fly fish, or even throw artificials, a tower in the middle of the cockpit is an annoying and unsightly encumbrance, not to mention the bad behavior the tower sometimes spawns. Looking for fish on plane has become an obsession of too many anglers, and they ruin everybody's fishing with their ceaseless high speed patrol of every grass flat in Tampa Bay — even those posted at idle speed.

Push poles still afford excellent control and maximum stealth on the flats and in backcountry bayous.

Fish the Flats

I also wonder about the push poles I see on 20-foot skiffs with 200 hp outboards hanging off the stern. I can't image what they are used for, other than staking out. If 10 years of pushing a boat with a pole has taught me anything, it's that every ounce counts. Anything over 18 feet and 150 hp makes the push pole an expensive ornament, not to mention the weight of three or four 70 pound 12 volt batteries and a couple or three trolling motors. Who are these guys kidding with the push pole?

Push poles vary in quality and price. I have owned several– a top-of-the-line, one- piece fiberglass pole and a less expensive replacement I bought when the former slipped off the boat unseen in rough seas. At one time, the lost pole was covered with name and address stickers, but they had long since peeled off or faded beyond legibility. When someone found that $300 pole, they had no chance of knowing who it belonged to, which gave me virtually no chance of getting it back. When I bought the new pole, I engraved my name and phone number in the plastic foot of the pole – which at least gives an honest person a chance to do the right thing.

The big difference between the cheapest pole and the best is going to be weight. However, added stiffness often comes with the weight, and that can be good or bad. I happen to like the extra stiffness of my new pole. To compensate

Fish the Flats

for weight, I opted for 18 feet of length instead of 20. The extra two feet is seldom missed, because much of the poling I do is in very shallow water. The shorter, stiffer pole also stays in the holders a lot better, but as it turned out, I am still able to bounce the pole off the boat in a chop.

On a last minute charter a couple of weeks after I lost the expensive pole, I filled in for a boat that broke down in a multiple boat charter. The other boats were headed to the mouth of the bay for tarpon, so I pounded my way through a big chop on a 12 mile run with my little boat. When we got there, one of the clients asked me "Did we lose our pole?"

Sure enough, the brackets were empty, the new pole was gone, and with paying customers aboard, going back to look for it is out of the question. Dang! That was my second pole lost in as many months. This time, I had my name and phone number on it. And sure enough, a week later I get a call from a guy who keeps his boat at Bahia Beach Marina – same place I was putting in at the time. He found my pole in the middle of the bay, saw the name and number on it, and tracked me down.

The moral of this story is if your name isn't on the pole, you have no chance of getting it back. And if your pole is not secured to the skiff in rough water, it can escape. I now have a release strap in place, (a short piece of rope that connects to

37

Fish the Flats

the pole) so that if the pole jumps off unseen, it's still tethered to the boat. Even with your name on the pole, it doesn't guarantee that an honest guy will pick it up. Somebody found a $300 push pole out there, and had no way of returning it, even if they were so inclined. Shame on me for losing that one, and for almost losing another. The lesson is to tie your pole down when you're running in chop, and have your name and phone number engraved on the foot.

With ever increasing regulations that prohibit running the shallows on plane, poling skiffs are likely to rebound in popularity if anybody ever gets around to enforcing existing law. In any event, poling a flats skiff will always be a superior way to fish with anglers who know how to cast. The only way to improve on the stealth of a poling skiff is to get off the boat and wade.

Trailer Maintenance

Getting a boat to and from the launch is something many fishermen take for granted, but for those who travel far and often, a boat trailer is integral part of fishing. As proprietor of a bait shop with a boat ramp, I get to see lots of trailers of all kinds, and some of them are downright scary. I have seen several trailers meet their end on the ramp, some falling apart during

38

launch, some before, and some after. And judging by the number of trailers one sees on the roadside, there are an even greater number of trailers that never make it this far.

Aluminum trailers are less susceptible to the corrosive effects of salt water, but not impervious, especially when galvanized hardware is mixed with stainless steel and fastened to aluminum. Galvanized washers used with stainless steel bolts and nuts create electrolysis that causes aluminum to erode at the point of contact. A trailer should not come from the manufacturer like that, but it happens, and the only way you can tell is through routine maintenance.

Trailer axles and hubs are generally made of steel, and while rust and corrosion are inevitable, a coat of paint when they're new and a fresh water rinse after each use will extend the life of both. Hubs also require a fresh shot of marine grease every so often – at least once a year — if you own a boat trailer, you need also to own a grease gun. I do not replace bearings or races. Instead I replace the entire hub every two years.

Trailer lights are also prone to fail, and my solution has been to replace them with detachable lights. These are inexpensive, and they can be kept out of the weather any time they are not in use, which means they will usually work. Lights that are fixed to the trailer should be disconnected before backing down the ramp. Hot

39

Fish the Flats

bulbs may break if suddenly submerged in cold water.

Another useful trailer accessory is the Rite On device. It consists of two magnetic wands with day glo tips. One is affixed to the trailer just behind the trailer's ball fitting, while the other is placed behind the trailer ball. Line up the two wands in the rear view mirror and bring them together and the ball winds up exactly where it's supposed to be under the trailer. This not only saves time, it eliminates relying on clueless helpers who couldn't guide water into a funnel, no less help direct the ball under the trailer. It was invented and is being marketed by Tampa resident, Capt. Bill Rentz (813) 245 1576.

Trailer tires seldom fail from wear. The real culprit here is most often dry rot – a common occurrence because most boats simply don't get enough use. If your boat is more than a couple of years old and it sits a long time between trips, a careful inspection of tires and hubs is wanted. Grinding hubs will be difficult to hear from the inside the vehicle, so have someone else back the trailer down the ramp every so often so you can listen for signs of wear.

It's a good idea to disassemble the hubs once a year to inspect the bearings and the races. Then if you buy and carry a spare set, you will have some idea of how to change them out. The other

40

Fish the Flats

good thing about the yearly routine inspection is that by removing the lug nuts, you can also re coat them with anti-seize compound while you're at it. That way should you have a flat tire, you'll be able to remove the lugs. For a simple flat tire from a puncture, there is nothing quite as convenient as having a can of tire inflator on hand. Who wants to fool with a jack in the dark on a 70 mph interstate where everybody is doing 90?

The most serious failures usually occur with steel trailers and galvanized trailers used in salt water. Often these trailers rust from the inside out and it's difficult to see how bad the corrosion is. The only thing you can do is rinse the trailer thoroughly after each use and inspect it closely and often. Aluminum trailers are also subject to corrosion and wear and tear. If cracks appear in any of the welds, they should of course, be repaired or the whole trailer can come out of alignment.

My trailer came equipped with black rubber rollers. When they finally wore out I replaced them with non marring yellow plastic rollers with solid, stainless steel axles – more expensive, but a lot more durable, too. I doubt that I will have to do that job again any time soon. However the first time I launched the boat with the new rollers it slid off the trailer prematurely, so take care if you make modifications to rollers or bunks. Speaking of bunks, they are often made of wood

41

Fish the Flats

and covered with carpet, and as such, are also subject to rot. You can check to see if the bunks are still solid by sticking them with the point of a knife – if it penetrates past the tip of the point, you know you've got a problem.

You will never appreciate how much you take your boat trailer for granted until you're stuck on the side of the road while everyone else is headed to the ramp. Routine maintenance and inspection is the best way to avoid trailer trouble, while maintaining the value of your package at

Power Pole Simplifies
Accurate Boat Position
Poling up on a school of redfish in clear shal-

Fish the Flats

low water with the wind at your back is tricky business. Same thing applies to approaching a big snook cruising a mangrove shore. Get a tad too close and the fish will blow out. And while you may be able to stop the boat with the push pole, holding position and making a cast at the same time is nearly impossible.

John Oliverio of JL Marine Systems, Inc. located in Brandon, Florida grappled with the problem and after five years of development came up with a solution, and dubbed the product of his ingenuity the Power-Pole. He calls it a shallow water anchor, and it's basically a hydraulically powered stake out device– a fiberglass stake on a hinged aluminum arm that reaches down to the bottom in up to six feet of water providing instant braking and superb holding power. Lifetime warranty on the fiberglass spike and built-in safety devices assure the owner years of reliable, trouble free operation.

In flats fishing, boat position is paramount. For evidence look to the professional Redfish Tour currently traveling through Florida, Louisiana, and Texas. To finish in the money, a Power Pole is practically required equipment. One of the foremost teams, twin brothers Greg and Bryan Watts credit their success to their ability to go extremely shallow, and to maintaining precise boat position through use of the Power Pole. In a 2001 field that averaged 100 boats, they fin-

43

Fish the Flats

ished in the top ten six times, and won the Championship event.

Anyone fishing from a flats skiff in shallow water will quickly recognize how important boat position is in maintaining a comfortable distance from the fish. Being able to stop the skiff in a matter of seconds with the push of a button is an incredible advantage.

Getting a boat into position to make the good cast means taking wind and current into account, and once you get the boat where it needs to be, it has to stay there. Wind is ever a primary concern. Always try to fish with the wind at your back; particularly when chucking live baits that do not cast inherently well. The tools I use most to secure the boat are my anchor and my Power Pole. Keeping the boat secured at two points prevents it from swinging in wind, waves or current. The characteristics of a good anchor are that it secure the boat quickly with a minimum of scope, and then hold that position.

All anchors are not created equal, and those that are designed to hook and hold generally cost a lot more than those built for the cost conscious. Many Tampa Bay guides employ anchors which have large bronze flukes on stainless steel shanks. This anchor does not require a length of noisy, fish spooking chain to help it set. When the bottom is soft, and too deep for the Power Pole, I stake out with my push pole.

44

Fish the Flats

Precise Boat Positioning for Flats and Backcountry Fishing.

Catching fish in shallow water calls for precise placement of baits or lures for most of the species we pursue in Florida. This is as nervous an environment for large game fish as it is for smaller fish at the bottom of the food chain. It calls for long, accurate casts into a strike zone that is seldom more than three feet for flats predators. If your boat is out of position, no amount of casting skill can make up for it. Capt. Chet Jennings of Tampa Bay goes to great lengths to put his boat exactly where it has to be. To get there he sometimes uses a push pole, and other times he will get off the boat and push

45

Fish the Flats

it into place. Then he might get off the boat and readjust position several more times according to changes in wind or current. Ten feet is often the difference between fishing and catching.

The line attached to the anchor should be soft and supple and long enough to hold in the deepest water you fish. A stainless steel shackle attached to a thimble into the anchor line makes the best connection; secure the shackle bolt with stainless steel wire so that it can't work loose.

For staking out with the push pole, I have a snap shackle attached to a short length of line tied to the poling platform. It attaches to the foot of the pole, and also serves as a safety strap for the pole when running. I once lost two poles in a matter of a couple of weeks that bounced off the boat while running in a heavy chop. That led to the installation of the safety strap, albeit a couple of poles late.

Naturally, I try to pole downwind. Poling into the wind is about as effective as trying to cast into it. I have a trolling motor, but still prefer the stealth of the pole; the added advantage of height of the poling platform let's me see exactly where I need the boat to be in relationship to the spot I'm trying to fish.

Boat position is equally important when throwing the net for bait, especially when chumming. If the boat is swinging two and fro, it's

46

nearly impossible to put the chum in one spot. Again, I like the boat secured bow and stern. This lets me chum the bait into a compact area where I can put the horn on the center of the slick and catch the most bait with the fewest throws of the net. If the boat is swinging back and forth on the anchor line, it's much harder to concentrate the bait, and that means more throws of the net, which in turn means getting wet, and getting the boat dirty.

47

Fish the Flats

Fish the Flats

Chapter 4

Catching and Keeping Live Bait

If catching the most fish possible is the order of the day, chumming live baits is the best approach. This calls for a live well full of scaled sardines, which are also called greenbacks, pilchards, and whitebait. With bait shop prices at 5 dollars a dozen and up, buying 800 to a thousand sardines is not an option for most. Nor will a sabiki rig fill the well fast enough if chumming the flats is the plan of battle. To catch large numbers of baitfish quickly a cast net is wanted.

Many fishing guides throw 10 and 12 foot nets to catch the most baits possible in the shortest time. Because they throw these nets practi-

Fish the Flats

cally every day, it's second nature. But the average angler doesn't need as much bait and doesn't need to throw that big a net. For most an eight-foot net with 3/8-inch mesh will catch most of what you need. Larger mesh nets may sink faster, and catch bait better in water deeper than eight feet, but it will also catch threadfin herring when they intermingle with pilchards. Mixing the two baits in your live well is not desirable. Threadfins are not hardy, and they shed lots of scale which can kill *all* the baits in the well.

My 3/8 inch mesh net seems to allow the faster, less desirable threadfins to escape, and that's a good thing if you are targeting pilchards. Nets smaller than eight feet might also do the trick, but it will take more time to catch the bait, and that time is subtracted directly from that allotted to fishing. Much also depends on the time of year, as well as the size of the baits. One net will not cover every situation., and serious live bait fishermen may own three or four nets: quarter inch mesh for small baits in shallow water, three eigths for average pilchards, and a half inch net for big baits in deep water.

A little hands on instruction is helpful if you don't know how to throw a net, and there are several good videos that will show you how to get the thing to open. Mostly it's a matter of learning how to load the net and coordinate body

50

mechanics. The best place to practice is over grass on dry ground. Having someone there to watch and help make the necessary corrections in form will greatly shorten the learning curve in cast net throwing. Learning to throw the net is the easy part; learning where to find bait on a given day is apt to take a lot longer, and here an understanding of the bait's lifecyle is important.

To keep large quantities of bait alive requires a functional, well designed live well system. Just because a boat comes equipped with a well doesn't mean it will work as intended. My first boat had a big bait well, but the 360-gallon per hour pump installed at the factory couldn't keep more than a few dozen pilchards alive for more than a minute or two. I replaced it with a 700 gallon per hour cartridge pump, and an aeration attachment. That solved the problem of keeping bait alive, and it made replacing the pump a simple chore when it fails. With regular use, pumps seldom last more than one year.

An oval or round shape is preferred for live wells with constant flow of fresh, aerated water. Timer switches that automatically turn the pump on and off work well and they minimize battery drain. Another desirable accessory is a high-speed pickup — a bronze through hull fitting that will automatically change the water out in the live well while the boat is on plane. Make sure there's a check valve between the thru hull

Fish the Flats

and the live well to prevent back flushing.

Capt. Chet Jennings transfers baits from the net into the bait pan. Unwanted baits and flotsam are quickly removed, and then the bait is dumped into the live well. This insures miminal handling and less stress for the baits, and doesn't make a mess of the boat.

Even the best live well wont make up for poor bait handling. Capt. Chet Jennings of Tampa Bay has it down to a routine. He stores his custom cast net in a large, flat plastic bin with a lid. After a good throw, the bait is transferred to the plastic bin, so unwanted baits, shells, sea weed and other debris that might clog the live well drains can be quickly picked out before dumping the baits into the well. This is much

Fish the Flats

preferred to unloading the net directly into the well, or dumping the baits on the deck where each has to be handled individually.

Mixing pilchards and threadfins in the same well sometimes kills both. Jennings theorizes that the shedding of small scales by the threadfins suffocates the pilchards, and threadfins are just not hardy enough to keep in quantity. Threadfin herring are a plentiful summer bait, but they are fragile. You can't pack 'em in a live well like you can pilchards, nor do they survive on the hook as well, but they do make a good cut bait for redfish and Spanish mackerel. Pinfish and chubs could survive in stagnant pool, and both are very hearty, but you can't chum with them.

After catching bait, give the bait bin a good rinse, and shake gilled baits out of the net. A lid

Fish the Flats

for the bin keeps direct sunlight off the net, which will prolong its life. An occasional quick dip in fresh water treated with a capful of fabric softener will keep the net supple, but don't overdo it. A capful in the bait bin, a short soak, and a good freshwater rinse is all that's required every couple of months. Tears and holes will pop up with regular use, and these should be repaired professionally on quality nets. With a cheap net, simply knot the holes closed, but the net won't open as well as it once did.

Chumming for Pilchards and Pinfish

Most of the time, I like to see some bait, or signs of bait before I start chumming, unless I have reliable information that there is bait in a given location. Sometimes you can see bait dimpling the surface, or perhaps even flipping out of the water. The large schools of bait that matt the surface and make a noisy commotion during the summer months are usually threadfins.

Pilchards will sometimes school on the surface in shallow water, but they present a more subtle disturbance than threadfins. Deep diving pelicans that throw their heads back after the dive are generally feeding on pilchards. Those birds making shallow dives that are more parallel to the water are generally eating glass minnows. Sea gulls landing on the pelican's head

54

also indicates that glass minnows are the target, same thing if the pelican seems to strain water out of its beak before throwing his head up to swallow. Pelicans and cormorants sitting on the water are always worth investigating.

Around deep water structures, such as range markers, you can generally see the bait. If it is right on the surface, I may not even bother to chum, but if I see it flashing four or five feet down, I will carefully position the boat with the anchors so I can chum the pilchards away from the structure to throw the net on them.

The old standard for bait chum was a mixture of wheat bread, saltwater, and jack mackerel or catfood. More recently, many West Coast guides use fish meal. I prefer the meal for its simplicity – just mix it into a paste with some saltwater and feed it out in marble sized globs. Other guides add menhaden oil, anise oil, and jack mackerel as extra attractants. Any recipe that draws the bait into the slick will do. The idea is to get all the bait you need with the fewest number of throws.

Finding and catching the bait is the hard part, but keeping it alive all day also requires some thought and preparation. I like to cull threadfins and pinfish before dumping the bait bin into the well as I pick out sea grass, shells, small blue crabs, skipjacks, and anything else that's not going on the hook. I am also very care-

Fish the Flats

ful about keeping my hands, and my client's hands and their kids' hands out of the live-well. Sunscreen, gasoline, oil, and insect repellent, may kill every bait in the well for days to come. Sea grass and other flotsam can clog live well drains and restrict the flow of fresh sea water and air that are necessary to keep large numbers of baits frisky and thriving.

Even if your hands were clean, chasing baits around with a bare hand is stressful for baitfish, and you want them lively as can be – always dip the baits out of the well with a net.

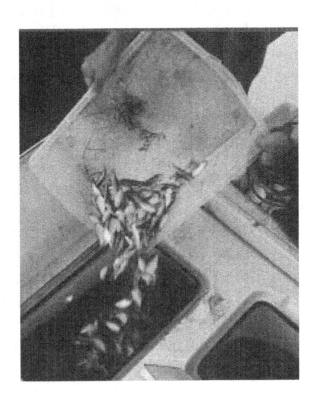

56

Fish the Flats

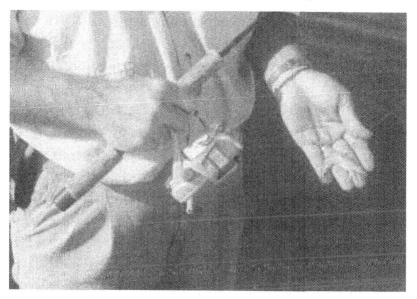

Chapter 5

Natural Baits – Dead or Alive

Shrimp

Shrimp are the most readliy available bait for flats fishing in West Central Florida because fishy predators relish them as much as humans do. They are relatively inexpensive and you can buy them live or frozen in most bait shops. They are available year round, with the best range of sizes occurring late fall to and early spring. Just about everything that swims, walks or crawls will eat a shrimp.

Snook fishermen prefer the large selects and jumbo shrimp because they cast better, while those who fish for mangrove snapper and sheepshead like the little ones, or even pieces of shrimp. Redfish anglers will often spice up a bucktail jig with a segment of shrimp tail.

There are many ways to hook a shrimp, but the two most important things to remember when fishing with live shrimp is to match the size of the hook to the shrimp, and avoid hooking live shrimp through the black spot in the head, which will instantly kill the bait. The horn, or carapace is the toughest part of the shrimp, and a #1 short-shanked live bait hook passed through the chin, or side to side ahead of the black spot will do the trick. Another specialty shrimp rig for tailing redfish is to bite the fan off the tail, and hook the shrimp just ahead of the severed fan. This allows a slow retrieve with minimal line twist. The same method can also be used with a jig head when fishing shrimp deep for snook, or for sight casting to cobia.

Shrimp are easier to keep alive than baitfish because they require less oxygen. Fresh water will kill them pretty quick, however, so anglers who fish brackish water with low salinity will sometimes keep them on ice folded in damp newspapers or paper towels.

Most bait shops buy their shrimp in lots of a thousand, randomly sized, directly from the shrimpers who catch them in the Gulf of Mexico. The better shops sort them and sell them by size.

58

Fish the Flats

Since most anglers prefer to fish with large shrimp, the selects and the larges are often sold out before mid morning. – big shrimp are seldom available in the afternoon, particularly on the weekends. Size is less important to game fish; bigger shrimp cast better, and that's their primary advantage.

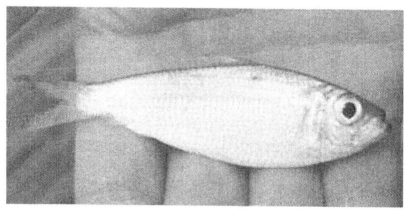

Pilchards

For anglers who catch their own bait with cast nets, pilchards are the staple of West Coast Florida flats fishing. Some knowledge of the pilchard's lifecycle is important in knowing how, when and where to catch them. These baits are also called greenbacks, scaled sardines, and whitebait.

Big pilchards school up on the flats toward the end of February on Tampa Bay. These are the perfect sized three to four inch baits that cast well and live a long time on the hook. The spawn doesn't take place all at once, and it continues on into late spring and early summer. Then suddenly the big baits disappear from the shallows, soon to be replaced by a much smaller crop. In a normal year, June through September, most of the bait on the flats is too small to fish with. Once the baits grow to two and three inches, I throw a quarter inch net on them to avoid gilling small baits. Big baits can be sometimes be found in deeper water, around structure. For example, bait can be had pretty much all year long around the pilings at the mouth of Tampa Bay – even when there is nothing on the flats. To catch bait in deep water with strong currents, a larger mesh net is wanted – ½ inch or 7/8 inch mesh.

Sometimes, however, bait will get trapped in the bay in the fall. A sudden and prolonged drop in water temperature in late October or early November usually means pilchards will stay inside the bay throughout the winter months. That's a happy occasion for fishermen, but not generally the norm. Pilchards also seem to be cyclic, varying in abundance from year to year.

Pilchards are most often fished live. When fished under a float or free-lined, the best place to hook them is right through the nostril. If you pass the hook through the right spot in the bait's nose, it is about impossible to fling it off. Here is where those chemically sharpened hooks are actually worth the expense. The pilchard's nostril is much easier to find with an extra sharp hook point, and I am equally certain that these points improve hook-ups.

When sea gulls and terns are molesting hooked pilchards on the surface, baits can be hooked in the belly and free-lined to make them run deeper. This is also a good way to chum a few baits down deep and out of the reach of sea birds. Simply cast the bait out, let it run a few yards with the bail open, then close the bail and rip the bait off the hook with a sharp jerk of the rod tip. When fishing belly rigged baits, it's best to let them be, as they will not survive cast and retrieve very well.

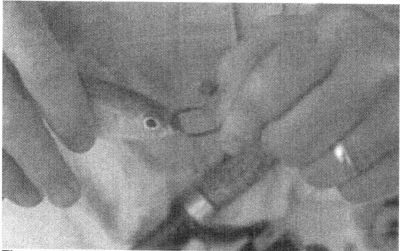

The nostril provides a convenient spot to hook a pilchard. It's hard to see, but a sharp hook will pass through with little resistance.

Fish the Flats

The top bait is a pilchard -- also called scaled sardine, whitebait and greenback. It is the bait of choice for snook, redfish, and trout. The bottom bait is a threadfin herring. At a glance the difference between the two is negligible. But look at the eyes; the pupil of the eye of the top bait is twice the size that of the lower bait. Note the black spot behind the gill cover on the lower bait. But the ultimate giveaway on the threadfin is the filament behind the dorsal fin -- hence the name. Both baits are effective, but the pilchard is stronger -- more durable in the live well and on the hook.

Threadfin Herring

Threadfin herring are plentiful from April through October, and at a glance they look like pilchards, but they are more fragile. You can't pack 'em in a live well, nor do they survive on the hook as well. The pupil of the threadfin's eye is much smaller than that of the pilchard, and it has a long filament trailing behind its dorsal fin – hence the name. Threadfin readily shed scales and are much harder to keep alive in num-

Fish the Flats

bers big enough to chum with. Many are the predators that feast on threadfin herring, from ladyfish, to cobia, to mackerel, to tarpon, not to mention snook and redfish and jack crevalle. A cast net is the most productive way to fill a live well, but they do not respond to chum like sardines, and they are good at getting out from under the net – especially in deep water. Guides who want big threadfins often employ a 12-foot net with a 1/2-inch mesh.

Threadfin herring also make great cut bait when fresh. I have tried freezing them a number of times, but the bait is mushy when thawed, and hard to keep on the hook. I like to have a few dozen threadfin on ice when fishing for redfish in the summer months. I cut them in half inch steaks with a filet knife and bait them on half ounce jig heads so I can pitch them into holes in the mangroves accurately. Snook will also readily eat chunks cut threadfin.

Chumming with small pieces of threadfin is also very productive for Spanish mackerel, and mangrove snapper. I like to get on the down current side of a range marker, and feed the chunks out in twenty second intervals until I see some fish in the slick. Then it becomes a matter of merely putting a hook in a bait and drifting it back to the feeding fish.

63

Fish the Flats

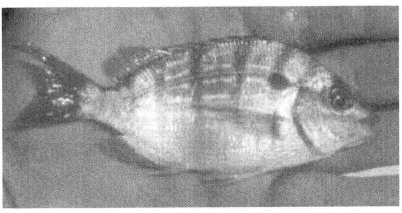

Pinfish

Pinfish are rugged baits. They keep forever in a good live well, and they can take abuse on the hook. Redfish, trout and snook will all eat pinfish, but size is important. Trout and redfish prefer smaller pinfish – those between the size of a quarter and a half dollar coin are about right for trout and reds. Snook will readily eat palm-sized pinfish, and cobia seem to prefer them above all other baits. For the shore bound fisherman who relies on a bait bucket, pinfish are the best choice because they travel better than pilchards and are very hearty – they can survive a long time in a pail of water with no aeration.

I usually gut hook pinfish. The nostril hook up does not seem to be as secure as it is with pilchards, and they are more active when hooked in the belly. Overall, they are hardier in the live well than they are on the hook.

Fish the Flats

Chubs

Shrimp, pilchards and pinfish are what you will find most often in the bait shops, but game fish are way less fussy about what they will eat than fishermen are about what kind of bait they will buy. Take chubs for example. These are very good bait for snook and redfish and they are available all year. Chubs are easily netted, they will keep in a bucket of water, and they are tough on the hook. Chubs are particularly good bait for flounder, snook and redfish, especially for snook in deep, fast moving water. I will also fish chubs on winter flats when other baits are hard to come by, and redfish, flounder and trout are equally willing to eat them.

Croakers

Croakers also fall into the category of underused baits. Large croakers are particularly good bait for big snook, and redfish will also readily eat one. I have also caught cobia on croakers, and I'm sure that most other game fish will swallow a croaker if it passes through the strike zone. I usually catch croakers in my cast net when I am trying to catch pinfish, and they are always a welcome addition to the bait well.

65

Fish the Flats

Grunts

Grunts are another extremely good snook bait. They look something like a pinfish, but they aren't as prickly and they do indeed grunt when put on a hook. For predators, the grunting translates to "Eat me! Eat me!" Grunts are usually caught on hook and line with a sabiki. Hand sized grunts are a preferred bait for big snook.

Mullet

Everything eats mullet. They are fished whole or as cut bait. Those who target trophy snook often fish big live mullet or mullet heads. Finger mullet are great baits formost gamefish on the flats.

Crabs

Most inshore game fish eat crabs, and certain species specialize in them. The Latin name for cobia means crab eater. Redfish and snook will often feast on small blue crabs, mangrove crabs, and fiddler crabs. Black drum, sheepshead, pompano, and permit are all crab eaters, too. Dollar sized blue crabs are highly prized as tarpon baits. All of the aforementioned crabs are very hearty, but beware of blue crabs of any size.

66

Fish the Flats

Even the small ones have sharp, powerful claws that will hurt you. Live crabs are usually fished without the claws, hooked through the corner of the carapace.

Ladyfish

Ladyfish are a great bait for a number of flats predators that includes snook, tarpon, cobia, jack crevalle, and sharks. Those who fish for monster snook will use whole, foot-long live ladyfish. Ditto for tarpon and shark anglers. Chunked ladyfish will also catch all of the above, and they freeze well. Ladyfish are also good gamefish in their own right. They are soft mouthed and accomplished aerialists, and very strong for their size – a perfect target for light spinning gear or a fly rod.

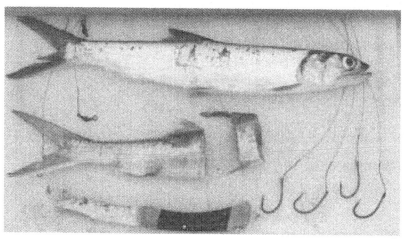

Fish the Flats

Capt. Nick Winger chums for pilchards at daybreak on the Southshore flats of Tampa Bay.

Fish the Flats

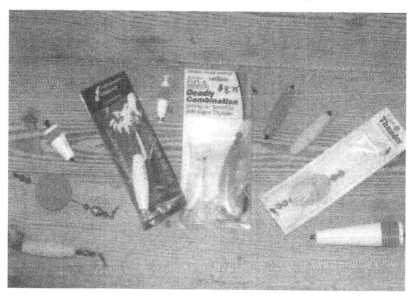

Chapter 6

Fishing with Floats

Floats are popular with flats fishermen and fishing guides for several good reasons: they keep baits from burrowing into sea grass, they provide a visual indication of where the bait is at all times, they serve as strike indicators, and they increase casting distance. Some floats make noise to attract the attention of predators, which is particularly effective on trout. Some do it with rattles, others with concave heads that splash and plop.

Some floats are weighted to improve casting distance, which is ever an important consideration in shallow water flats fishing. Many of the fish we pursue on the flats are ambush predators. Snook and trout are opportunistic feeders that will not move more than a couple of feet to strike a bait. And with small, light baits such as shrimp and pilchards, it is practically impossible to cast them far enough without adding weight. A float adds weight but still lets the bait swim freely — anchor a bait to the bottom with a sinker and the fish most likely to find it will probably have whiskers.

I make my own baseball sized round floats weighted with half ounce egg sinkers. They cast well, they are highly visible, and even big baits can't pull them under.

The problem with weighted floats is that they tend to outrun the bait during the cast. The result is that sometimes the leader crosses over the line behind the float during flight, and the end product is a tangle above the float. The remedy is a smooth cast, and a minimal length of leader. Casting a weighted float into the wind makes the problem worse, so I always try to fish with the wind at my back – a good rule of thumb no matter what you have tied to the end of your line.

Floats equipped with plastic and metal rattles are popular with trout fishermen because they are effective. A trout float can't make too much noise, and trout respond to the rattle like

70

it's a dinner bell. The float technique for trout is to jerk the rod tip sharply to make it splash and rattle. Redfish and jack crevalle will also respond to the noise. However, when I am fishing for snook, I prefer to let the float sit still.

In bright light, fluorescent pink and neon yellow are the easiest colors for me to see. In low light or overcast, dayglow orange seems to stand out best.

Popping corks were once the rule on the flats, and they are still popular. The concave top of the float makes a popping sound and a splash when jerked. The problem with that is that the float will also create drag when you are trying get the line tight on a strike. But that's a personal opinion – many flats anglers still prefer popping corks.

A new style of floats have evolved that slide on stiff wire. Because the float has some play on the wire instead of being tied or pegged directly to the line, hook sets are quick and sure. The disadvantage is that this float must be tied on, and the only way to adjust the depth of the bait is to shorten or lengthen the leader, which means retying.

Floats that are slit down one side may be pegged onto the line, and depth is easily adjusted. When using big baits that have enough weight to cast well, this float is a good choice, but it won't cast as far with a small pilchard or a regular

71

Fish the Flats

shrimp.

When fishing shallow water mangrove shoreline, I like to use a float to keep track of where the bait is. A free-lined pilchard will seek the shelter and security of the roots, and snag the hook in the process. With a float, I can see when the bait is getting too close to structure, or too far from where it has to be to catch fish.

Below the float I tie 30 inches of 30 pound monofilament, and a 1/0 L141G Eagle Claw Kahle hook if I am fishing with baitfish. For shrimp I prefer a 9174 Mustad #1 live bait hook. Where I fish on the Southshore of Tampa Bay, I am seldom concerned about altering depth.

If you are fishing with more than two anglers it's much easier to keep an eye on where all lines rigged with floats. I like to use big floats that the bait can't pull under. This way when the float does go down, I know that it's a hit. I think that not being able to pull the float under also keeps the baitfish in a state of panic, which is enticing to finned predators.

When the float goes down let it stay under for a two count, point the rod tip at it and reel fast as you can until you can feel weight. Then come up with the rod tip – a short, sideways tug is more effective than a full bore, lip ripping hook-set.

Fish the Flats

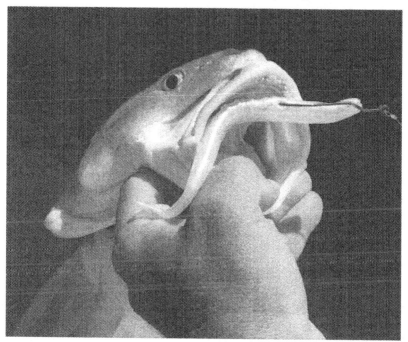

Chapter 7

Artificials

Soft plastic baits have revolutionized flats fishing with artificials. These baits look incredibly lifelike, and they can be impregnated with stuff that makes them smell and taste like the real McCoy. They come in an infinite variety of shapes and sizes, some are pre-rigged with hooks, but most are not.

I think the biggest advantages of soft plastics are that they can be rigged truly weedless, and they are incredibly lifelike in appearance. The weedless option gives fishermen access to

73

Fish the Flats

weed choked water where no bare hook would dare go, and this is often where the lunkers lurk – particularly when you're talking snook, trout, or redfish.

My favorite bait for shallow-water, summer fishing is the jerk bait, of which there are many brands on the market. All will catch fish. I throw RipTide's Flats Chub when targeting snook, but this bait has caught plenty of redfish, trout, jack crevalle, cobia, and even flounder. And when I say shallow water, I mean less than 24 inches deep. Here I prefer to fish the jerk bait without any added weight. Fish in water this skinny are usually edgy; they will often spook on the sound of heavy lures plopping into the water if they land less than five feet away. I also find that weight impedes the sharp, darting action of the jerk bait.

There are many styles of worm hooks that allow a jerk bait to be rigged weedless, just be sure to avoid cheap, light-wire hooks made for fresh water bass fishing. Snook and redfish will effortlessly straighten hooks that are not up to snuff – even on 10 pound test line. I am sorry to say I know that from experience, but it only had to happen once before I sought a stronger hook.

I am ever experimenting with different styles of worm hooks, looking for the perfect companion to the jerk bait. Currently I like the keeper hooks for ease of rigging. The keeper attached to the hook eye makes it easy to get the bait to dart through the water when the point of the hook comes through the belly of the bait in the right spot. You don't want the bait to turn screws through the water, as this will cause line twist and deter strikes.

The point of the hook should be started into the bait where the deepest part of the bend of the hook intersects the bait. Then the point should be driven perpendicular to the back of the bait and then turned into the groove. The point of the hook should rest just below the top of the groove so that it makes instant contact with the fish when it strikes. The bait should lie in a straight line with the leader when hung between the fingers. I also like True Turn Brute hooks for their good point and sheer strength. These hooks are slightly harder to rig, and the baits do not hold up as well as they do on the keeper hooks, but they are very sure on hook sets. The Brutes get their great strength from forged bronze construction, but that also means they will rust. On the other hand, they are inexpensive, so replacing them is no big deal.

Capt. Chet Jennings likes Eagle Claw lazer sharp worm hooks. He tells me the point is very good, and that he is impressed with consistent hook ups. I'm sure there are many good worm hooks, and there are apt to be many more new and improved hooks to come. The three most important things to consider are overall strength

75

Fish the Flats

of the hook, a design that lets the bait run true, and a point that hooks and holds saltwater tough flats fish. Price should not be an important consideration. Think about what everything else related to flats fishing costs.

Artifical Shrimp

There are many soft plastic shrimp on the market, and Mark Nichols' DOA shrimp is first and foremost for good reason. It looks and smells like a real shrimp, it comes in a variety of colors, and it flat out catches fish. However, fishing the DOA shrimp is very much the same thing as fishing with live shrimp. This bait is most effective when drifted through the water column – so it is something of an oxymoron for the artificial bait angler because it's very much like fishing live bait. But in certain situations, the plastic shrimp is the perfect choice.

A good example would be a swift, deepwater current along a rocky shoreline. Here the plastic shrimp will drift with the current much as a live shrimp would do, without hanging up in the rocks as a jig is apt to. Another good application for the plastic shrimp would be site casting to fish laid up on mangrove shoreline. This is a low impact bait that you can put in the fish's face without spooking it. I have caught several nice snook this way, they turn on the bait, look at it

Fish the Flats

for a fraction of a second and then pounce. That's about as exciting a hook-up as a take on a top water plug.

I have caught snook on the DOA shrimp, and also on the RipTide Realistic Shrimp, and I am sure that most of the other artificial shrimp will catch fish when placed in the hands of an angler who has confidence in that particular bait. The point being that a plastic shrimp is an effective lure that should have a place in every tackle box on the flats.

The Plastic Crab

Some fish on the flats prefer crustaceans above all else. Permit, pompano, and black drum are examples that come to mind. But most fish will eat a small crab, and if crabs are what's there

77

Fish the Flats

and what the fish are eating, it's hard to get them to eat anything else. Tailing redfish are another example. The redfish with its tail in the air is not looking for pilchards, pinfish, or finger mullet – it's after something in a shell.

I had a graphic illustration of that on the Southshore flats of Tampa Bay one fine spring day in two feet of gin clear water. I was poling clients across a shallow water flat under a cloudless sky, late morning with the sun high. I spotted a school of redfish heading toward the boat, so I put my Power Pole down, chummed a few live baits and then put a pair of pilchards on floats out in front of the school. As the red fish surrounded the floats I was surprised that none of them hit the chummed pilchards, no less so much as sniff at the baits on the hooks. In desperation, I threw a gold spoon into their midst and let it sink to the bottom. Then I gave a sharp jerk of the rod tip, which created a puff of sand . A redfish charged the spoon from 10 feet away and whacked it. Another cast with another gold spoon and my clients had two fish on, yet not one boil ever came on the chummed baits, or those on the hook under the floats. These fish were obviously eating something off the bottom, and when I gutted them back at the dock, turns out they were full of small white clams. What the gold spoon had in common with the clam is only speculation, but my guess is the fish keyed on

78

the way the spoons puffed out of the sand.

When fish get single minded about what they eat, they key on the special of the day, and won't eat anything else. So it is when they are eating crabs. If you don't have a crab or a crab imitation in the box, anything else is likely to be ignored.

Size is important, and with redfish and snook, I like the two inch baits. RipTide has a very good blue crab imitation in a few different colors. It's primarily a winter bait for me, because that's when we have the extreme low tides that afford good sight fishing opportunities. Redfish are off the grass, cruising over bare sandy bottom, so the exposed jig hook is not a concern. There is also very little to choose from on the winter flats in the way of forage, except for crabs and finger mullet. and I expect crabs are easier for redfish to catch than mullet.

I don't give the crab any action. I pitch it beyond the fish and crawl it across the sand with a slow, steady retrieve. The strike on the crab is usually subtle -- the line comes tight and it feels like the jig is hung up. When that happens, I give the rod tip a sharp sideways tug and usually hook up.

Fish the Flats

Hard Baits

Besides the array of soft plastics, my box includes several hard baits. Mirrolure's Top Dog Jr. is and Heddon's Super Spook are my favorite topwater lures. I like to throw the surface plugs for big snook and redfish around sunrise and sunset, and after dark.

Both plugs are designed for the "walking the dog" retrieve, a darting effect where the plug changes direction every time you pop it with the rod tip. The plugs are equipped with rattles which add an intriguing sound that accompanies the splash and gurgle of the plug as it's retrieved. Surface strikes are generally explosive. For colors, I like red and white, and chartreuse and gold. Capt. Bryan Watts says he likes to fish the red and white in low light, and the flashier colors in bright water.

Another plug that Capt. Greg Watts encouraged me to try was the 7MR. One day in December while poling up on schools of redfish with my friend Robert Derick of Vermont, we made numerous casts into big pods of redfish with spoons and jigs with no results. Then I tied on a gold and chartreuse 7MR, and we hooked and landed six fish in the next hour. When redfish repeatedly refuse any lure, it's time to switch. Who knows what triggers their preference? The day before the same school of fish on the same tide, with all conditions identical, readily hit red jig heads with root beer tails. Go figure. But if you know the fish are there, and they won't hit one lure, try another.

I also like to throw surface plugs at jack crevalles, but I work them differently. Here the retrieve is as fast as I can reel with the rod tip pointed at the lure. The strikes are incredible.

Spoons

Any selection of flats lures for Tampa Bay

Fish the Flats

would be incomplete without an assortment of spoons. Capt. C. A. Richardson gave me a handful of Capt. Mike's spoons several years ago, and they have been regulars in my tackle box ever since. The 3/8 ounce white spoon is the number one selling lure in my bait shop, and for good reason -- it catches a wide variety of fish, it casts well, and it's weed resistent .

Known primarily as go-to lures for redfish, I have caught snook, cobia, jacks, and even flounder on Capt. Mike's White Spoon. Sometimes I rig a plastic tail on the single hook.This keeps the spoon higher in the water column and also helps it shed weeds.

Because weeds seem to be ever present on Tampa Bay, all of the spoons in my box are now single hooked with weed guards, but I have also caught plenty of fish on treble hooks, and on many other name brand and off brand spoons.

One problem with any spoon is that it is apt to cause line twist. I minimize this characteristic by installing a barrel swivel on the spoon, and if spoons are the order of the day, I tie in a barrel swivel between leader and line. The double swivel arrangement seems to relegate line twist to an absolute minimum.

The great thing about fishing any spoon is that it's easy to work. You can vary retrieve between slow and steady or give it a jerky action by popping the rod tip gently to make it flash

82

like an injured baitfish.

I have come to rely on white as the primary color, but I still carry gold and silver spoons in my box, mostly in quarter ounce and 3/8 ounce.

Lead Headed Jigs

If an angler was restricted to only a single lure, the leaded headed jig would be tough to argue with. Practically every predator with fins will hit a jig.

On the flats of Tampa Bay, the most important consideration in any jig head is hook strength. Jig heads with good hooks cost two or three times what those with light wire hooks do, but since the jig is one of the least expensive, most effective lures, why skimp? The very best jigs cost little more than a dollar each. When compared to the price of a top of the line plug, skimping on jig quality is an error that trophy fish will make you pay for.

Finish on the head is also a consideration - - not so much for it's fish catching ability, but its angler appeal. I fish a good looking jig head with more confidence than one that's beat up.

For durability and effectiveness, real buck tail is hard to argue with. Yellow, and red and white bucktails will catch just about everything that swims.

Plastic tails designed to be rigged on jigs

come in a variety of shapes and sizes and colors. I like to match to color of the jig head to the tail in terms of brightness. For example, in dark, tannin stained water I would fish a red head with a root beer colored tail. In bright clear water on a sunny day, I prefer a white jig head and a bright tail, such as chartreuse, gold metal flake, or pure white.

I carry three sizes of jig heads. Quarter ounce for calm days, shallow water and slack current, 3/8 ounce jigs for deeper water and gentle current, and half ounce heads for deep water that's moving. When the wind is blowing, the heavier heads cast better.

I match my retrieve to conditions, varying the speed according to where I find fish in the water column. Sometimes this takes a while to figure out, but there is seldom a situation where a jig is absolutely ineffective.

And that rounds out my conservative lure selection. I would rather carry a very small selection of proven lures than conduct an endless hunt for the latest catch all gizmo as advertized on TV. If you don't have confidence in a lure, you won't fish it hard enough to catch fish on a slow bite.

Chapter 8

Casting and Rod Handling Skills

Making long accurate casts is essential in shallow water fishing. The closer you are to the fish, the greater his chances of seeing you, and catching fish that know you're there is a tough proposition. If the fish is too close he might spook on your casting motion, bail flip, or any other slight noise you might make. A 120-foot cast is minimal for routine success especially when fishing from a boat, and while it's not that far, sometimes it has to be done with baits and lures that don't cast inherently well.

To get the required distance calls for care-

85

Fish the Flats

fully matched tackle — the right size reel spooled with supple line that comes off the spool easily, on a rod whose action is matched to your lure selection.

The mechanics of a good cast begins with loading the rod. The idea is to sweep the rod backwards with the forearm with enough force to flex the rod. Then drive the rod forward using the forearm and the wrist to generate tip speed. A light rod with some flex in the tip may be cast with one hand: a heavier, stiffer rod with a fast tip may require both hands.

To drive a one handed cast snap the wrist forward at the end of the forearm stroke. Accuracy is achieved by minimizing arm motion -- more like short chop with a small hatchet than throwing a ball. A big sweep of the arm will not generate enough tip speed to achieve maximum distance, and it also impedes accuracy. Make the rod do the work with an economy of motion,use the forearm and the wrist for a short, compact stroke, and finish it off with the rod tip pointing slightly above the top of the arc of the line. You can actually hear the difference between an efficient cast, and a poor one. The latter makes more noise, because the line is chattering through the guides slapping the blank. Line hums off the spool on an efficient cast . The hand holding the reel should not move much more than a foot during the cast, and it shouldn't travel

Fish the Flats

behind your shoulder. Finish off the stroke with the arm and the rod extented toward the target.

Close the bail just as the lure hits the water. Most bails will close easily with a turn of the reel handle, but pushing it over with your fingers is a better habit to aquire. When you crank the bail closed, it sometimes picks up slack and leaves one of those nasty little loops in your line. At best a burried loop is sure to reduce casting distance; at worst it will cause an annoying bird's nest that eats up your line and your fishing time. Cranking the bail closed makes more noise, and stealth on the flats is everything.

The motion of the two handed cast is still like chopping wood, but with a bigger axe. Propel the cast by pulling with the bottom hand and pushing with the reel hand. Again, it's a short stroke that's finished with the rod tip pointed above the target.

Spinning tackle is easier to master than bait casting tackle, but both have their place in flats fishing. The best way to attain maximum casting accuracy is to fish artificials often. Casting distance and accuracy is an acquired skill. The more casts you make the better you'll get.

When casting to fish I can see, I try to throw my lure or bait beyond the fish, but in front of it. Then I try to ease it into the three-foot strike zone, keeping the rod tip high in the air and as

87

Fish the Flats

much line off the water as possible.

On a visual strike, resist the temptation to set the hook until the lure disappears and there's felt weight – a difficult thing to do when you see the hit. Lip ripping hook sets are not necessary for most fish. Rod jerks will miss more fish than they hook. A short, sideways tug is what I prefer for a hook-set and that's all it takes. Even with my whippy rods, chemically sharpened hooks penetrate and set well.

Once a fish is hooked and taking drag bring the rod tip up and keep the pressure on. Reeling while a fish is taking line causes twist, and does nothing to bring the fish to heel. Pressure the fish toward you by lifting the rod -- take line with the reel as you lower the tip, then lift the rod tip again. This is called pumping the rod -- you take line with the reel only when the fish will give it, and play the fish with the rod, not haul it in with the reel.

If the fish heads for roots or structure, feather the spool of spinning reels with the fore- finger to add drag. On bait casting reels, addi- tional pressure can be applied by thumbing the spool. Drag pressure on any reel should be pre- set according to what line is spooled. This set- ting is a matter of experience, tempered by feel. It can also be done with a scale. Be very careful with drag sets on extra strength lines that may exceed the limits of the rod. For example, if the

88

Fish the Flats

rod is rated for 15 pound test line, and you spool 30 pound superline, your drag should still be set for 15 pound line. If not, something has to give, and it could be your rod.

The best way to land a fish is to play it out away from the boat. Let the fish run, but maintain constant, relentless pressure. When the fish turns comes your way, relax. Maintain pressure and keep the line tight. When fish run at you, reel like crazy and try to maintain pressure. You may not keep up and slack line may occur. Keep reeling. If the fish is off, you have nothing to lose. If you can catch back up and get the line tight , you've still got a shot at landing the fish. The longer the line stays slack, the better the chance the hook will pull. You don't want to horse the fish , but don't let it rest and recover strength.

Once a fish is whipped and coming to the boat leave a rod's length of line between the fish and the rod tip. Sit down with the rod tip up in the air and grab the leader with your free hand, put the rod down and deal with the fish. Reel the fish too close to the rod tip and bad things may happen. You may break your rod, or lose the fish because you can't reach it.

Unless I intend to kill a fish, I prefer not to use a net. Redfish, snook and trout become docile soon as you can get a hand under their belly. If you lip a snook, he will try to rip your arm out

89

Fish the Flats

of the socket. Sticking your thumb in the mouth of redfish or trout will make you bleed. Don't handle fish you are going to release with a towel, or dry hands. The slime that covers the fish is a barrier against bacteria, and you want to leave it intact. Buy a de-hooking tool and learn to use it for catch and release. The tool also keeps hands and fingers out of harms way of catfish spines, shark teeth, stingray barbs and other dangerous appendages.

A hook remover will hands and fingers out of harm's way and makes for a quick, clean release of fish not intended for the table.

90

Fish the Flats

Everybody likes to take photographs of big fish, and there is a right way and a wrong way to go about it. Holding a big fish vertically is putting its internal organs in a most unnatural position. Far better to support the middle of the fish with one hand, using a lip grip to support the head. It's best to keep fingers out from under the gill covers, especially when handling snook, which have a sharp edge on their gill plates. If you are going to take several pictures be sure to keep dunking the fish.

Releasing the fish should be the most rewarding part of the outing. The best advice is to hold the fish steady in the water until it recovers on its own. Don't drag the fish backwards through the water — gills don't work this way.

91

Fish the Flats

This snook was over the top of the 26 to 34 inch slot. It swam off after resting a minute. Such fish are the brood stock that produce future generations of snook, and must be handled carefully if y our grandchildren are to know the joys of snook fishing. Such fish are way too important to be caught just once.

Fish the Flats

Chapter 9

Wade Fishing

It's ironic that an angler fishing on foot has a leg up on the guy fishing from the high dollar, shallow-water skiff. Reason being, the guy on foot presents a much smaller profile and makes less noise. And some anglers who own boats, even the expensive, hi tech shallow draft hulls — use their boats mainly as transportation.

As a veteran grouse hunter used to plodding mile upon mile through the hills of Vermont, fishing on foot has an inherent appeal. Indeed, stalking the flats on foot is very like hunting the edges of timber for birds and the best thing about wading the flats is that there are no hills

93

Fish the Flats

to climb, and here it's seldom too cold to fish.

The beauty of wading is its simplicity, especially when fishing artificial lures. When I first abandoned ship, I waded in old sneakers with a bag of jerk baits, a package of worm hooks and a couple of pieces of leader material. The results were immediate, and suddenly I was catching more fish and bigger fish than I ever had before.

Beautiful as simplicity may be, it will only take you so far, and as I started to specialize in wading I began to customize my approach. The first piece of wading equipment I bought was a pair of neoprene flats boots. The soles are thick and the fit is snug enough to keep sand out. Nor will the boots suck off your feet in soft mucky bottom. Today there are several wade boots marketed especially for flats fishing. Ultimately, comfort and protection from most things sharp should be the primary considerations.

The second piece of gear I bought was a fanny pack. This let me carry a small selection of lures, a camera, a bottle of water, a container of insect repellent, and some sunscreen.

That was years ago. Now there are several companies that market wade belts with multiple rod holders, stringers, and storage compartments. I have the Wade Aid belt made of closed cell foam encased in neoprene. It comes equipped with three rod holders, a stringer, a box for tackle, and forceps. The belt is lightweight,

94

comfortable, and offers some much needed back support. Check it out on the internet at Wadeaid.com

Basics

I am spoiled by the very good wading that the Southshore of Tampa Bay affords. Here we have mostly hard, sandy bottom and much of the wading I do is in water less than knee deep. For me, the ideal tide to wade on is the extreme low tide that accompanies the new moon and the full moon. Less water means that fish must concentrate in the limited space of the deeper holes. It also means that the troughs and the swash channels are easier to see, and this is where game fish will congregate to feed.

Also, moving fish are visible on the flats at low tide. Redfish feeding on the bottom during an extreme low tide often expose the tips of their tails while pushing their noses around in the sand, which makes for an exciting site fishing opportunity.

Snook will also show themselves on the flats at low tide. They don't tail like redfish do, but sometimes they will make a wake while cruising in shallow water or their yellow fins will poke through the surface. Snook usually swim in straight lines; they move faster than mullet, and baitfish will generally part the sea in front of a

95

Fish the Flats

snook on the move. Other times snook give themselves up with a loud pop of the jaws as they strike at baitfish. Put a lure near the scene of the crime, and it's gonna get hit.

Hazards

The first question I'm asked about wading when I do seminars is usually "Aren't you worried about sharks?"

Sure, there are plenty of sharks around, and some of them are big enough to hurt you, but I wouldn't give them much thought unless I was trailing a stringer full of fish. For that reason I don't do it. If I catch a fish I want to eat when wading, I hoof it right back to the boat.

Nope. Sharks are not much of a threat. Stingrays are another matter. They are ever present on most flats, and if you step on them, they will whack you. I have been stung three times, and I'm not sure a shark bite could hurt more. I know all about the stingray shuffle, but when I see a yellow fin waking its way out of casting range I tend to march.

My fishing buddy, Capt. Chet Jennings has been wading for 20 years, and has never been stung, so it also has something to do with me being a stingray magnet. Popular radio show host Capt. Mel Berman got stung on one of my "Snook Soirees", only because I hadn't got off the

96

boat yet. Otherwise I'm sure the ray would have found me first.

Fortunately the antidote for this painful wound is a dab of meat tenderizer followed by a one and a half hour soak in very hot water. Then see a doctor for a tetanus shot, and make sure none of the barb remains in the wound. The sooner you get the sting in hot water, the sooner the pain will subside. It takes about a half hour to really get rolling, and the pain can be severe and incapacitating, so get off the water fast.

After stingrays, the stuff that's most apt to make you bleed while wading are oyster shells, rusty nails and broken glass. If you fish live bait, hard head catfish can also put you in a world of pain should one fin you during hook removal. Meat tenderizer will minimize the experience, so it's a good thing to have handy .

Strategy

I like long, limber rods that will cast a six inch jerk bait 40 yards on ten pound test line for open water flats fishing. Experimentation with a variety of blanks has led me to 8 ½ foot six weight fly rod blanks, tied up as spinning rods with five inch butt corks. I enjoy fishing these rods on open water because they cast so well, and they are fun to play fish on.

My tide preference for wading is the last

97

Fish the Flats

two hours of the fall and the first two hours of the rise. A change of tide that occurs around sunset is perfect. When the sun hits the St. Pete Skyline at the end of a falling tide, the water usually starts to boil with strikes. Snook, redfish and trout all become active.

In general, I fish for snook on the falling tide, and redfish and trout on the rise. On a good evening, you can get the slam several times over.

Reading the water is easiest on minus tides. Swash channels and cuts are apparent when the water is shallow in the extreme. To pick the best days to wade fish, you need a comprehensive tide chart for your area – one that gives you tide heights and peak flow as well as times. The days around the full moon and the new moon offer the greatest range of water movement, and these are called Spring Tides. The weaker tides on the half moon phase are called Neap Tides.

I like to cast upcurrent in swashes and retrieve the lure with the current. This is the way that bait travels, so it's the most natural presentation.

My go to lure here is RipTide's six inch jerk bait in pearl glow, but I also like Mirrolure's 7MR and Top Dog Jr., Captain Mike's white spoons, and 3/8 ounce jig heads and curly tails – bright colors for clear water, and dark colors for muck. Knowing what to throw is dictated by water conditions and what mood the fish are in. I carry

Fish the Flats

a minimal selection of lures that cover the water column from top to bottom, and just try to figure out what the fish want by changing lures and varying the speed of retrieve until I start getting strikes.

The best places to catch fish on the flats are those spots where the current flows strongest. Creek mouths, swash channels and cuts through sand bars are where game fish like snook redfish and trout are going to stage.

You can tell where the current runs strongest by observing the surface of the water. There will be a rippled effect where the most flow is. Ambush predators like snook and trout are going to set up along the edges of the flow to pick off baits as they are swept by with the tide.

Redfish and tend to rove more than snook

99

Fish the Flats

or trout. In summer time they bunch up in small schools at low tide. Sometimes you will see them tailing, but seeing is not always catching. Tailing redfish are after crabs and shrimp; they will usually refuse baitfish and baitfish imitations when shellfish are on the menu. Here I like to throw RipTide's two- inch plastic crab, and sometimes a spoon, or a jig head and grub tail. When casting to tailing redfish, it's important to get the lure on the bottom where the fish can see it, then make a slow retrieve.

A pearl colored jerk bait is a snook thumper in warm, weedy water. You could drag this bait through a bowl of spinach and still catch fish with it. Use a stout hook and rig it in line so that it darts from side to side when twitched with the rod tip. It's most effective in very shallow water.

100

Fish the Flats

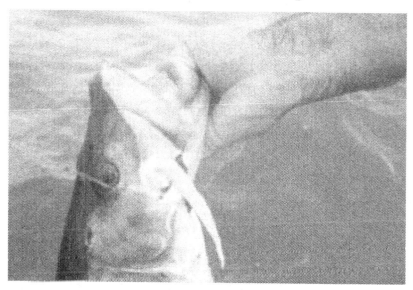

Chapter 10

A Flats Lure for All Seasons

"I don't know what they think it looks like," said my friend as we walked across the flat. "It doesn't look like anything. Maybe a needlefish."

And to see the white, soft plastic jerk bait dangling from the tip of my long rod in mid air I could hardly disagree. But it does its work in the water. It caught 100 snook for me in two months the first year I started using it.

The bait is six inches long, something like a rubber worm, except fatter, firmer, and

101

Fish the Flats

straighter. In the water, when rigged right, it will dart side to side –like walking the dog with a plug. I believe its darting action triggers fish to whack it.

Besides action, other characteristic of the jerk bait that make it ideal for shallow water flats fishing is stealth. You can cast it very near a fish without spooking it, because the light plastic bait hits the water with such a little splash that fish think it's real bait flicking the surface.

Snook, redfish, big trout and jacks all hit it with gusto. I have tried several brands; 12-Fathom Slam 'R''s, Mister Twisters, and the six-inch Riptide Jerk Baits. One of my friends even caught a big flounder on one. So whatever it looks like to us, to fish it obviously looks like something to eat. I fished the same white bait for four months on the flats of Tampa Bay. What a treat not to worry about having to switch lures. About the only change I make in the bait is to sometimes add weight by inserting a finish nail into the head. This makes it cast better when it's windy, and will sink the lure faster where you need to fish it deeper.

When I started fishing these baits, I picked my hooks at random – using whatever was on the pegboard in the store I happened to be in. This did not pose a problem until I began to hook some bigger fish. When a big snook turned on a bait with the swirl and swoosh of a trophy, I was

102

able to stop the fish after its first run, but then the line suddenly went slack. The freshwater hook had straightened. I had told myself the 10-pound test line would part before the hook straightened, and I was dead wrong. I started using high dollar premium hooks -- extra strong 4/0 and 5/0 are what's wanted for tough customers like snook, bull reds, and jacks. Bronze hooks seem to be strongest, but are prone to rust. Some of the new chemically sharpened worm hooks are so fine, it's hard to keep them from making me bleed.

Recently I have enjoyed good succes on redfish with jerk baits rigged on Capt. Mike's weighted hooks. The mouth of the bait is threaded onto a wire keeper attactched to the eye of the hook, and there's a lead weight cast onto the hook shank just below the eye. The red finish on the hook doesn't hold up well, but it gives the most consistent hook sets I've ever had on redfish and trout. For snook I still prefer an unweighted hook.

Another thing I experimented with in conjunction with the jerk baits was flourocarbon leader material. A sales rep for a fishing tackle wholesaler gave me a spool of 25-pound test Triple Fish flourocarbon to try. The first thing I noticed was that it seemed stiffer and harder than monofilament, and it resisted abrasion well. But the selling feature of flourocarbon is low visibil-

103

Fish the Flats

ity once it's in the water. I had never tried it before because it was so pricey – costing four times as much as monofilament leader material, but now I am convinced it makes a difference. At around $18 for a 50 yard spool of 25# test, it works out to about 20 cents for an 18 inch leader, which is hardly unreasonable. Especially when a bag of 10 jerk baits is less than four bucks. The flourocarbon leader material is a little harder to tie, which is the only other drawback I see.

Jerk baits will cause line twist, even when rigged properly. I connect leader to line with a uni knot; careful to trim the tag ends close to the knot to minimize weed fouling. I tie the same knot to the hook, leaving a small loop to enhance lure movement. The standard Texas rig is ideal for fishing weedy summer flats, but care should be taken to rig the bait in line with the hook, otherwise it will corkscrew through the water, twisting your fishing line and deterring strikes. I push the hook point into the bait where the mouth would be, and then bring it out through the chin a quarter of an inch down. The hardest part to get right is gauging where to insert the hook point a second time in the belly of the bait. Too far back and the point will lie buried in plastic where it will miss fish. too far up and the bait will sag between the eye and the bend of the hook, which will cause the bait to spin instead of dart. If the bait doesn't look right, re-rig it until it's

Fish the Flats

straight.

The soft plastic bait is tougher than it looks. I have caught up to four snook on a single bait. The first part to tear out is where it is hooked in the head. When that happens, I bite half an inch of the head off and re-rig the bait. You can do this a couple of times. As long a bait darts in the water, I will continue to use it.

This weedless rigged bait allows you to make those productive casts right into the tangle of mangrove roots, or into the middle of a patch of saw grass. With the hook point sheathed in plastic, this is a very forgiving lure – much moreso than three sets of naked treble hooks.

Another big advantage of the jerk bait is its nearly neutral buoyancy. This means that once you get the bait into the sweet spot in the shadows and the cuts, you can keep it in there a long time, fishing it very slowly with slight jerks of the rod tip. The violence of the strikes the jerk bait draws in the shadows is often shocking.

Most of the fishing I do with this bait is in shallow water. I prefer to get off the boat and wade when the water depth is about knee deep. If it's deeper than that, I fish from the boat. I have had my best luck fishing jerk baits for snook and reds in water less than two feet deep.

Wade fishing is pretty simple with jerk baits. You can carry a pack of hooks and some spare leader material right in the zip lock bag

105

the baits come in and carry that in your back pocket. I tend to range far from the boat once I go over the side, so I have a fanny pack that has a couple of compartments, and a water bottle. I carry a couple of bags of baits, hooks, leader material, a spare spool, sunscreen, bug dope, and a stringer.

When fishing in clear shallow water, you should also consider what you wear to avoid spooking fish. White hats and shirts are alarming to fish. Sky blue or green are colors that will blend you in with your backround better from the fish's eye view. Polarized sunglasses are essential to cut the surface glare of the water to judge the best lies, and to actually see the fish.

I have been able to make the most of fishing jerk baits because I fish with long, light custom rods that cast these baits well, but a seven-foot spinning rod with a moderately fast action will do. I like more flex in the rod tip for casting jerk baits. Hook setting is over-rated on the flats. In fact, I heard one prominent snook guide give a seminar where he repeated over and over, "Never set the hook on snook!" I agree, especially when fishing jerk baits. The Riptide baits are scented and flavored, and my experience has been that fish hang onto them a long time. Just point the rod tip at the fish and reel on the strike.

The obvious places to fish jerk baits on the flats for snook are the cuts in the mangrove shore-

106

line, oyster bars, and over grass. Snook hiding in the grass on an open flat are not there to relax. To enter that hazardous environment where they themselves could get eaten by a porpoise or a shark means they are hungry. I pay particular attention to large patches of grass near creek mouths, and gaps in the shoreline where the current flow will be exaggerated.

Redfish seem to prefer a mixture of sand patches and sea grass. They are every bit as wary as snook, and may even be harder to entice with plastic.   The flourocarbon seems to be even more important with redfish, which paradoxically are not supposed to see as well. Can't prove it by me.

Trout are most often found in the deeper water on the outside edge of the grass. The specks I have been catching on the six-inch baits are mostly bigger trout, 18 inches and over. Smaller trout have a harder time ingesting six inches of plastic.

If you enjoy fishing artificials and you haven't learned to fish the versatile, effective jerk bait yet, you are missing out. I used to figure the lead headed jig was the best lure ever devised, but I don't go to them as much as I used to. Being able to skip a bait into those tight spots, deep in the shadows, with small chance of getting hung up is a huge advantage. Not having to change lures to accommodate different species is another.

Fish the Flats

Chapter 10

Give the jerk bait a thorough try out and I am sure you'll get hooked.

Jerk baits are equally effective on redfish as they are on snook, but darker colors seem to draw more strikes from the reds. If the fish are tailing, I use a weighted worm hook, such as Capt. Mike's Keeper hook, to get the bait on the bottom.

A 3/16ths ounce lead weight gets the hook where the fish can see the lure. I try not to drop the bait too close to the fish, and cast into sand holes where it will be easily seen. Even weedless rigs are not totally foul proof, and if you can move the bait a few feet through a pot hole, it will usually draw strikes.

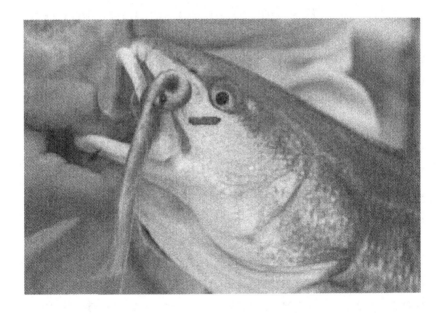

108

Chapter 11

Spotted Sea Trout

A favorite of Florida flats fishermen, spotted seas trout are some of the prettiest fish found in saltwater. They do indeed resemble freshwater trout, replete with spots. But soon as the trout opens his mouth revealing a set of long canine teeth, the similarity ends. Also called specks, sea trout are aggressive fish that are found on the flats all year long. They are closely related to weakfish, which are found in north-

109

Fish the Flats

ern waters, so called because they have a soft mouth -- a trait shared by sea trout.

You will find trout on the flats all year long, but peak fishing probably occurs in spring and fall. In general, they prefer deeper flats with turtle grass.

Trout are the least feisty of all the fish featured in this book, but gator trout -- those over two feet long -- are respectable fighters. Trout are also among the most aggressive fish on Florida's flats. They will readily hit an array of artificials, and are attracted to noise. Any lure that rattles and splashes is apt to draw strikes if you cast it in front of a trout. Highly regarded as food fish, many are the local anglers who target sea trout.

Big trout, are most active in low light situations. On some of my sunset wade fishing trips, gator trout can be found in ankle deep water making a racket like a pop corn machine as they tear through schools of bait.

Trout can be chummed into frenzy just like snook or redfish, but since they are so aggressive, most trout fishermen use lures. Tandem rigged Love Lure's are the standard in artificials, but if it's big trout you want, try a surface plug such as a Zara Spook or a Top Dog. My buddy Terry Ackroyd is a trout specialist. When he's hunting big trout, he throws Mirrolure's 52 MS, and other trout anglers have also touted the very same lure in my bait shop.

I have caught most of my trout on RipTide's jerk baits when fishing for snook and reds. I've also caught many trout while fishing with jigs. Pink, or chartreuse tails seem to draw the most attention.

My method for finding trout is to get on the poling platform and try to spot them in sandy potholes. When I start seeing a few fish, I put the Power Pole down and probe the surrounding area with long casts.

Trout like deeper water than redfish or snook during the day. I usually look for them in four or five feet of water over turtle grass. But around sunset, big trout can get very shallow. When an extreme low tide coincides with sunset, the action can be frantic.

Trout are considered to be among the best eating fish, but they require special care. If not iced immediately after they're, they tend to get mushy.

They are also delicate. If get on a school of 12 to 14 inch fish, I usually move on to another spot. Of all the fish we catch on the Tampa Bay flats, trout are probably the most fragile. They do not handle well, and playing catch and release with short trout on every cast is sure to be a death sentence for too many. Never put a dry hand or a towel on trout, and use a de hooker to maximize survival rates when targeting trout.

Fish the Flats

Because of their willingness to strike artificials trout are also a favorite of saltwater fly fishermen. Not as rambunctious as redfish, snook, or jacks, a seven weight fly fishing outfit is perfect. It will readily handle the largest trout you will ever catch, and provide good sport with the average fish. Shock tippets are not necessary for sea trout, but ladyfish are often present in trout habitat, so a 20 pound tippet might save a few flies.

Fish the Flats

Seasonal Tactics for Redfish

Summer

Midsummer flats fishing can be a bear for Florida fishermen, but there are a few stellar angling opportunities for those who can hack the heat. Redfish tend to scatter into the shade of mangrove roots for solace during the summer doldrums. Here they become harder to catch than when schooled up as they are in spring and fall. But redfish in the shadows will eat. The trick is to put the right bait where the fish can find it.

Capt. Nick Winger taught me this technique for catching big redfish in the heat of midsummer -- chumming and fishing with chunks of cut bait (threadfin herring or ladyfish).

In June, July and August look for redfish in deep cuts in mangrove shoreline on a slack high tide. Water clarity is generally poor due to algae and regular rainfall, so sight fishing is seldom an option. Hunt the deep holes along shady mangrove edges. Small passes that penetrate deep into the root structure are where redfish sulk in the heat of the day. It's possible to fish live baits here, and pinfish and pilchards can be productive, but free lined baits tangle in the roots -- they're difficult to cast in habitat that calls for precision in bait placment.

Nick's technique is to cast cut bait into the middle of a mangrove pocket and let it lay there. When a redfish finds it, the line comes tight as the fish tries to retreat into the shadows. Putting the brakes on this run is one of the great challenges in inshore angling. It's one of the few occasions where I worry about breaking rods. But when a fish can be held at the shadow line, I usually win the tug of war. If the red gets up a head of steam and takes drag, it's break-off city.

For casting precision I rig my cut bait on jig heads. The advantages are many. Threadfin herring are abundant on Tampa Bay in the summer months, and their frailty in the live well and on the hook becomes a non factor when you cut them into half inch steaks. They make an excel-

114

lent cut bait because they are oily and put out lots of scent. It's easy to fill a cast net with six inch baits on Tampa Bay, provided you can find the bait in shallow water. Water deeper than six feet however, calls for a big net that sinks fast. An eight foot net with 3/8 inch mesh is no match for threadfin in deep water, or in strong current. Here 10 or 12 foot nets with 7/8 inch mesh are a better choice. Pick baits out of the well as they die and put them on ice to keep them firm.

Initially, I fished the chunked bait on an ordinary live bait hook, weighting the leader with large splitshot, or with rubber core sinkers. This made for a clumsy casting arrangement, however, with way too many casts finding their way into the brush. My solution was to rig the cut bait on a jig head. I know, it sounds funky and it looks that way too, but it works. Jigs cast inherently well because the weight is at the extreme end of the leader. With a jig, I can pitch a piece of bait into that three foot opening to reach the deepest, darkest shadows where big reds like to hang out. Strength of the hook on the jig head is paramount.

The next problem with fishing in the roots is to get big fish coming your way the second you hook up. Twelve pound test monofilament on a short stiff rod is very minimal. This is an excellent application for 20 or 30 pound microfilament

Fish the Flats

line. It casts well, resists abrasion, and offers greater line strength for finer diameter. I also beef the two-foot leader up to 60 pound mono. The still water of the mangrove backcountry is often murky, and the leader is laying on the bottom, so visibility isn't as much of a concern as barnacle encrusted roots.

I use 7 1/2 foot heavy spinning rods rated for 30 pound test for redfish in root structure, and they have proven to be a pretty fair match – even for oversized fish. Even so, break offs happen. Given the nature of the habitat and the inherent strength of the redfish, there is no perfect choice for a rod. If the rod is too stiff, casting accuracy suffers and you can't put the bait where it needs to be – too limber, and it lacks the muscle to pry the fish away from the safety of the shadows.

Tides are important when fishing root structure. The higher the tide, the more apt the reds are to cruise the shadow line. I like the last hour of a big rising tide on a new moon or full moon. Time of day seems to be irrelevant. Some of my best days have come during the heat of midday on the last hour of a rising tide.

Chumming with cut bait is also productive. Cutting up a half dozen threadfins and loading them into an open ended wiffle ball bat, then flinging them around the shadow line can turn on a bite. Some of the reds we catch may have 20 or

116

Fish the Flats

thirty pieces of the cut bait in their bellies when we clean fish at the dock. Once you get them eating, these big reds cover the bottom like vacuum cleaners, sucking up every piece of bait they can put their nose on, whether it has a hook in it or not. The negative side of chumming is that sometimes it will draw the attention of large stingrays and catfish, so I chum sparingly, and then only when the bite is slow.

Boat position is critical. I try to keep my skiff a long cast away from where I think the reds will be. These fish are wary in the extreme to any sort of noise or motion. The farther you keep your bait from the boat, the better your luck is apt to be.

Another good case for heavier tackle is that you don't want to overly stress these fish. Big reds give their all, and you have to be careful in the heat of midsummer not to play these fish to death. Minimize handling of fish that are to be released, but hang onto them until they've had time to recover. I simply hold the fish upright with my hand under the belly until it swims off under its own power. I use a lip gripper and hook removing tool and never net a fish I do not intend to keep.

There is nothing easy about prying big redfish out of the roots. The mangrove backcountry can be extremely hot, and if the wind is light, or you are on the lee side of the mangroves, it can

117

Fish the Flats

be downright stifling. You'll want to apply plenty of sunscreen and drink lots of fluids. If you can stand the heat, and fish the right tides on the shadow lines of the mangrove backcountry, the reds of summer are often willing.

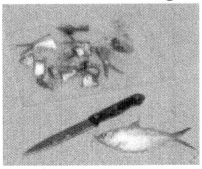

A rambunctious redfish puts on a topwater display.
Note the dark hole in the backround above Keli's right arm. This is where you put a bait to catch summer redfish.

Fish the Flats

Winter and Spring

Redfish are not as susceptible to cold water and cold weather as some of the our tropical species, such as snook. This makes them catchable, but because winter tides are low with tap water clarity, there is nothing easy about putting a hook into a red. Pilchards are apt to be scarce, so chumming live bait is seldom an option. And while redfish will seldom refuse a shrimp, getting the bait to the fish is a little more complicated. Small shrimp do not cast inherently well, and large select shrimp often create too much of a splash for sight casting. The redfish you find in shallow water are wary as any snook – and perhaps more so. This type of fishing requires ultimate stealth, so what's an angler to do?

If you would fish with shrimp for tailing redfish, the first thing to do is scale back the size of the shrimp. Medium and small shrimp will catch more fish in ten inches of clear water because you can cast them closer to the fish with less of a splash. The problem is that small shrimp do not cast very well. The solution is a longer, limber rod – 7 ½ foot is pretty minimal, and then spool up with lighter line. If you usually fish 10-pound test, spool down to eight, or even six-pound line, if your rod is limber enough to handle it. Winter flats fishing for redfish is no place for a short, stiff rod. When you need to cast a light bait far, it calls for some flex in the rod tip.

Another solution would be to put the bait under a small, weighted float. This will help you cast farther, but the float can't be cast too close to the fish, or it will spook them. When fishing live bait under a float in winter for reds, you need to put the bait well ahead of the fish, and let his nose lead him to it. Cast the float within six feet of a red in shallow water and it will probably vamoose.

The same rules apply to fishing for winter

Fish the Flats

reds with artificials. Sight casting to shallow water reds calls for precision. You need to do one of two things – cast the lure as far as you can throw it and work it carefully into the fish, or cast beyond a fish and bring it into his line of sight, taking care that you do not spook it with the line. That's another advantage of a long rod – with the tip extended high in the air, you can keep more line out of the water — line slapping the surface is often enough to spook the fish. For that reason when targeting redfish in gin clear water, I like to fish eight pound test monofilament. It's stealthier and casts farther. I like Ande's IGFA monofilament for this work

Another factor to consider in clear shallow water is lure color. On overcast days in murky water, dark colors are most productive. On

121

Fish the Flats

bright, sunny days in clear water, fish bright colors with lots of sparkle and flash. Some days will call for jigs hopped across the bottom, other days the fish like plastics fished close to the surface. If you are seeing fish, and they aren't hitting what you throw at them, by all means try something else. I've caught fish on dark colored jigs one day, and returned the next only to have them refuse the same bait. A change of color and depth, and suddenly the bite was good.

My winter lure selection for redfish includes six inch RipTide Flats Chubs on Capt Mike's weighted worm hooks. Hard baits would include Mirrolure Top Dog Jr's in chartreuse and red and white, and Mirrolure 7MR's in chartreuse and in gold. Quarter ounce RipTide jig heads with an assortment of different colored tails, and a couple of gold spoons will cover most of the bases for low water winter redfish. When possible, I prefer to wade, but long accurate casts from a quiet, shallow water skiff will also put fish on the line.

The two most recent additions to my small selection of artificials for winter redfish includes RipTide's two inch crab, and Capt. Mike's 3/8 ounce white spoon. When the fish have refused everything else, I've found they will usually eat the crab. It's a very effective lure in clear water over bare sand. I don't give the crab any action whatsoever -- I just drag it slowly across the sand, trying to mimic the crawl of a real crab. Weight

Fish the Flats

of the jig head depends on wind and water depth.

What About Fall?

Redfish are most plentiful and easiest to catch in the fall-- from late August through late October. They bunch up on the flats in large schools and feed aggressively. As long as a school of fish is not pressured by boat traffic, the reds will eat most anything.

Local guides like to chum 'em up with live sardines, and if they start eating them they will wear you out.

I prefer to pole around the school and work

123

Fish the Flats

the fish with artificials, and while that's not as productive as chumming, it's a lot more sporting. Mirrolure's Top Dog Jr., 7MR, Capt. Mike's White Spoons, Jerk Baits, and jigs are all effective.

The best tide to fish for schooled redfish is the low rise. They displace a lot of water when they're bunched up and sometimes you can see schools of redfish from great distances. I have seen them in clear shallow water so plentiful that a part of the flat was actually tinted in copper. These fish are more easily approached than smaller groups, and they tend to be very competitive trying to get at baits or lures.

This is also the time of year when big, bull reds invade Tampa Bay before heading offshore to spawn -- many fish are way over the 27 inch cap.

Fish the Flats

As with most anglers who come to Southwest Florida, the first fish I became enamored with was snook. My first book was basically a tribute to that great gamefish. But recently I find myself targeting redfish more than I do snook.

I suspect the reason is that slot size redfish are more plentiful than slot sized snook, but beyond that, redfish are tenacious fighters in their own right. A snook has more energy and is a stronger fish in the short run, but even big snook wear out quickly. Redfish have this incredible strength and endurance. One of the highlights of my fly fishing career was a 10 pound red on a seven weight fly rod. The big fish got well into my backing three times and took 15 minutes to land. I had no trouble releasing that fish. But because slot fish are plentiful, I feel no guilt about eating redfish on a fairly regular basis, though I prefer fish closer to the bottom of the 18 to 27 inch slot.

Redfish are also easier to find on the open water of the flats most of the year when the water is clear, and often too cold for snook. They have a much higher tolerance for cold water, and the chill doesn't seem to affect their strength or endurance.

Their willingness to take a variety of artificials is also an endearing trait, one that has made the redfish my new fish of choice.

125

Fish the Flats

Capt. Nick threw a live pilchard to this redfish while wading the mangrove backcountry on a high falling tide. Note the spots on the tail -- they supposedly imitate eyes to confuse predators.

126

Fish the Flats

Improve Your Success on Snook

You can catch snook on practically every stage of the tide, most of the time, if you know how the fish behave in a given location, but it's the hardest part of snook fishing to master. Some spots are good only on a falling tide, while others produce on the rise. Some spots require a high tide, others a low tide. Some locations produce lots of small fish, others produce the big torpedos. Keeping a log is the best way to collect data and analyze it, but if you can do it in your head, fine. However, most fishermen should resort to paper and pencil after each outing.

A tide chart is helpful only if you know how

127

Fish the Flats

to read it. Knowing when the tide is high or low is a small part of the equation. The best tides for snook fishing are those that move the most water, because the faster the flow of the current, the more bait that's carried with it.

Snook are ambush predators. They are not lazy, but very efficient. A hungry snook is going to lay up where current will pass a meal in front of his face. One look at a snook's broad, flat tail will tell you that this fish is built for a short burst of speed. A hungry snook may cross six feet of water to strike a bait, but don't count on it. Three feet is a more realistic appraisal of the snook's strike zone, and that's an axiom that applies to live bait as well as it does to artificials. If your bait doesn't pass within three feet of the snook's line of sight, it will likely ignore it to wait for an easier meal. It's not like the fish has places to go and things to do. If a snook picks the right spot and is patient, dinner will surely pass through the strike zone. An example of the "right spot" to fish for snook is a pass where current funnels through in a rush. Snook will lay up in the eddy. Creek mouths, swash channels, troughs, and change of depth around structure is where you look for snook. Snook fishing has many similarities to freshwater bass fishing, but the striped fish is a much tougher critter.

A snook in shallow water creates a commotion when it strikes a bait, and man is not the

Fish the Flats

only predator to key on the disturbance. I'm sure that porpoises also thrill to the sound of snook crashing and thrashing baitfish – good reason for the snook to pick and choose what, when, and where he eats. A snook is not showing off when it hits a bait — it's really out of character. Snook appear most relaxed when sulking in the shadows or stalking slowly across a flat like the assassins of the sea grass that they are.

I have caught more than one snook that gave himself up with a loud pop. On one occasion I waded about a hundred yards to the scene of a strike, and caught a 28 inch snook on the first cast where telltale bubbles on the surface gave the location away.

Capt. Bryan Watts caught a huge trophy snook in the same way on one our "Snook Soirees". I heard a strike more than a hundred yards away. Bryan was nearby, slid over and made a cast with a red and white Top Dog Jr., and the fish made a thunderous strike on the plug.

Fish Where They Are

Snook may like certain flats, certain oyster bars, potholes, and such, but things change. For the most part this is dictated by food supply, tide, season and fishing pressure. If a flat is covered with a variety of bait, chances are there will be snook in close proximity. World famous

129

Fish the Flats

Snook like to hang on the shadow line of the mangroves. The fish to the right of Keli's elbow was lurking in the dark, but came out to investigate Keli's bait. On a high tide look for snook in the shadows of the mangrove shoreline. Extreme low tides force them onto the flats where they generally seek cover in the grass.

snook guide Capt. Scott Moore preaches in his seminars that wherever you see glass minnows, there are bound to be snook. But because the bait was there a week ago, or even yesterday, doesn't mean it will be there tomorrow. And you don't need a tower to spot bait. Birds will wade on it, dive on it and follow it around. It will dimple the surface, and attract swirling predators. Learn to read the water with a critical eye. Look for the swash channels that cross through sand bars, and anything that increases the flow of current. Pay attention to the bait cycles, water tem-

130

Fish the Flats

perature (prime snook fishing occurs above 70 degrees and below 90), tides, and time of year and fish accordingly.

Snook can also be notoriously finicky, even professional guides have days when the snook simply won't bite. A two degree drop in water temperature will shut a snook bite down like the slamming of a door, even if the water temperature is in the 80's.

Generally, snook will feed with gusto ahead of a front, and shut down for a couple of days after it passes. Same scenario for hurricanes and tropical storms.

Falling barometer good bite, steady or rising barometer means slower fishing. Ron Taylor, Florida's West Coast snook expert at the Florida Marine Research Institute, tells me that snook will also seek the lee shores on windy days, just like fishermen do. And if the wind blows in one direction for several days, that also seems to turn the snook bite off

Snook Tackle

There is no such thing as an all around snook rod. Snook can vary in size from dinks to the big dogs, but it's the location you fish and the baits you use most that dictate your rod selection. On shallow water flats strive for long casts with low impact baits – i.e. soft plastics, small

131

Fish the Flats

jigs, spoons, live pilchards, and shrimp. This means longer rods (71/2 feet is minimal) and lighter line — ten pound test monofilament, or 20 pound braid will cast far with plenty of strength for open water snook fishing.

Around mangrove edges or dock pilings casting distance is less important than rod muscle. Here you want a shorter, stiffer stick that will throw short accurate casts and have the backbone to pull fish away from structure before they can use it to break you off. Fishing around deep water pilings in holes around river mouths and passes call for grouper tackle with the drags tightened all the way down.

Use at least of 18 inches of leader material of 25 pound minimum strength for open water flats fishing. Check it often for nicks and dings, and cut it back if it gets chafed when catching a snook. Two inches of chafed, milky leader in front of your lure or hook will deter strikes. Remember that a snook hunts with his eyes. Upgrade leader test to 40 or even 60 pounds around structure.

Confidence Lures

If you fish mostly artificials, cut your lure selection down to four or five proven lures. These should be baits you have confidence in through proven performance, or simple faith because you

Fish the Flats

like the way they work and look in the water. For example, I throw weedless RipTide Jerk baits in water that's less than knee deep. I will also throw a single hooked gold spoon with a weed guard in shallow water and bright light. In deeper water with lots of current, I will toss jigs between one quarter and one half ounce. In low light situations when weeds aren't a concern I like Mirrolure's Top Dog Jr. and 7MR. I don't throw much else. Other lures work for other anglers. The idea is to have confidence and faith in each and every lure you throw. The best means to that end is a small selection of productive lures. Just make sure all hooks are snook tough and extra sharp.

Cast Well

Last but not least, perfect your casting mechanics. Strive for the most distance and accuracy you're capable of. Remember, that lure has to hit a three foot target at distances of up to 120 feet and more on the flats. With shorter casts around structure you have to be able to thread the needle into channels through mangrove roots, and between dock pilings. Getting hung up is a big part of the snook fishing game. If you never pitch a bait into the trees, you're not fishing where the snook are.

133

Fish the Flats

Chapter 13

Perfect your fish fighting skills

Set your drag properly. Learn to feather the spool with your finger to add extra drag when you need it. Keep your rod tip up and make the rod do the work once the hook is set, and keep the pressure on. Forget that Saturday morning, cable TV lip-ripping hook set. A nice short tug of the rod tip is all that's required with a sharp hook, even with a long rod and a limber tip. If the snook runs to the right, pull the rod sideways to the left. Every time the snook changes direction, pull the opposite way with your rod. Never give a snook slack line. If the fish jumps, thrust the rod tip down, just like bowing to the king.

Live Baiting Snook

Chumming snook with live pilchards is effective on average fish, but less so on trophy sized snook. Guides who specialize in chumming snook spend time to net 500 or a thousand pilchards, most of which will be used for chum. It's possible to catch 20 or 30 snook and more on a good day, and you may even get a keeper, but the technique is best suited to guides who know where and how to catch that much bait. The individual angler can probably do well enough throwing artificials, provided that casting accuracy is sharp as it needs to be. Snook are ambush predators.

134

Fish the Flats

They set up in hide outs where current will sweep baits to them, and if you can put the right lure in that three foot strike zone, and fish the right stages of the tide, you can catch snook.

Those who target the big dogs, do so after dark with big baits such as ladyfish, croakers, grunts, and whole mullet. If it's big snook you're after, they are found in deeper water with lots of flow. River mouths, inlets, and passes with plenty of depth and current are where to hunt trophy snook. Cut bait is just as effective as live bait when targeting trophies. Big female snook are adept scavengers, and what could be an easier meal than a fresh chunk of ladyfish or mullet?

135

Fish the Flats

On extreme low tides, mature snook that live in the mangrove backcountry are forced onto the flats. Look for them on the outside edges of sandbars. These fish tend to hang in the drop off right next to the bars. I expect they avoid deeper water because of dolphins, which seem to have a decided preference for eating large snook.

Those who target big snook with artificials employ big lures. Large surface plugs are the ticket for low light conditions in shallow water, while long, lipped plugs with stout hooks are used around the deepwater structure of bridge pilings, and in deep, swiftwater passes.

In summary, snook are more affected by

136

Fish the Flats

changes in season than most of the other non-migratory species in West Central Florida. The snook is a truly tropical fish that is most active when water temperatures are above 70 degrees. A winter fishery does exist for snook in the northernmost extremes of its range, of which Tampa Bay is a part, but it is simply not the same rambunctious fish during the winter months, so I tend to leave them alone in December and January, or until the water temperature rises.

This snook ate a large chunk of ladyfish on a jig head rigged to a wire leader. It was meant for a blacktip shark that was cruising around the boat, but thesnook found it first. Big snook are scavengers.

Fish the Flats

Capt . Nick Winger slinging live pilchards over a snook hole -- a productive way to persuade finicky snook to bite.

Fish the Flats

Chapter 15

Cobia

My jaw gets tight when outdoor writers assign labels like dumb or lazy to different species of game fish. It has to make you wonder. After all, what could be dumber than demeaning any fish that helps you earn a living, whether you write about it, or try to catch it?

139

Fish the Flats

So when somebody tells me cobia are dumb fish, I grit my teeth. Aggressive? You bet. Fearless? That too. The adult cobia's position near the top of the food chain, and its size leave it with few natural predators other than the most dangerous species (anglers and sharks).

I love fishing for cobia. I spent many years fishing in fresh water where four pounds was a heavy fish. One of the cobia we caught last year had a four-pound stingray in his mouth, yet the fish hit a five-inch threadfin herring. Now that's big. And they get that way fast. A two year old cobia might weigh 25 pounds.

A cobia resembles a catfish with its flat head and wide mouth, but it zips through the water with incredible power and speed when hooked. Sometimes the fish will leap or dance on his tail, but a cobia's usual reaction to a hook set is to put it into overdrive. Few fish do it better.

If you were trolling offshore with heavy tackle, catching cobia would be fun. But finding a 40-pound fish in two feet of water when armed with flats tackle is an experience way beyond mere fun, it is one of the pinnacles of sport fishing.

Cobia often cruise the flats of West Central Florida in Spring and Fall. I once encountered a large cobia while wading a mangrove shoreline on high tide. Coming face to face with a big fish that looks a lot like a shark while you're

Fish the Flats

waist deep in water is not a recommended experience for the faint of heart. I reacted on impulse -- popping the fish in the fore head with the rod tip before I realized it wasn't a shark. It swam off unconcerned, and I didn't venture a cast. My flats rod was no match for a 50 inch cobia while fishing on foot.

Tom Rienhardt has this big cobia about worn out. In water this clear, Capt. Chet Jennings was able to spot the fish far from the boat.

Fish the Flats

Chapter 14

Cobia on the Flats

Besides sharks, there are two opportunities to tangle with oversized fish in shallow water on Tampa Bay. Tarpon is one and cobia is the other. When the sun is high and the wind is down, from late winter through early summer, cobia will cruise the flats, often in the company of large spotted eagle rays and big stingrays. This fishing is made to order for a tower boat, but on a calm day, large rays and individual cobia can be easily seen at a distance from deck level.

I am usually fishing in four feet of water with the outboard idling. Not only do cobia not seem to mind, sometimes the motor makes them outright curious. I have seen many cobia swim right up to the transom in the wake, and have even hooked a few there.

Cobia that travel with rays are in the feeding mode, but only accurate casts will draw strikes. Cast too close to the fish, and it will spook. Too far and it won't leave the ray to strike a live bait or a lure. The perfect cast is 10 feet in front of the cobia and 10 feet beyond -- lead the fish then time the retrieve so that it passes three or four feet in front of its nose. Make the first cast your best. I've hooked fish after mulitiple casts, but the hookup ratio on cobia soars if the first cast is on the money.

It's also important to maintain distance.

Fish the Flats

Spook the ray with the boat, and the cobia may refuse the bait. If the fish comes off the ray to take a look at the bait, keep it moving. The fish has to think the bait is trying to escape, which is why it's important to try to stay a long cast away. Sometimes you run out of room with the retrieve and the fish will break off the pursuit close to the boat. But if it doesn't take the lure and veers away, try throwing a different lure at it. I've had cobia miss a jig close to the boat, but hooked the same fish with a plug on the next cast.

The best time to hunt for cobia on the flats is when the wind is down and the sun is up, but the rays are so big and the water is so clear in spring and fall you can sometimes spot them in chop with overcast skies. Even a big cobia can be hard to see when riding with a ray, so I cast at most rays, particularly when visibility is low. Sometimes they travel beneath the ray, and all you might see is the fish's tail sticking out, so look sharp.

I like to use heavier tackle for these fish, which can weigh 60 pounds. I spool 12 pound Extra Strength Stren on a large capacity spinning reel, and tip it with three feet of 60# leader. A half ounce RipTide jig head rigged with a plastic tail will cast well and it gives sure hook ups. I avoid treble hooks for cobia. Blue crabs make up a large part of the cobia's diet, so the fish are subsequently hard mouthed. Single hooks offer

143

Fish the Flats

superior penetration, and they hold better than treble hooks.

If you are going to put the cobia in the boat, play the fish all the way out. A long handled sturdy gaff with a good point a better choice than a net. Just be sure the fish meets the minimum length before you strike (here in Florida it's 33 inches, measured to the fork of the tail). Fish that weigh more than thirty pounds are tough on net handles.

The Florida limit has also been reduced to one cobia per angler. I used a lip gripper on my last fish and it almost tore the handgrip off the tool, and my right arm out of its socket. I won't try that again.

One of the cobia's less endearing traits is the way it gets its second wind once it hits the deck. Until you experience 35 pounds of energized muscle thrashing around in the confines of the small cockpit of a flats skiff, you don't know what real mayhem is. Then there are those pointy little retractable spines that raise up out of the dorsal fin like a row of razor blades. I still bear scars on my left hand administered by my first cobia.

Food quality of this fish is said to be excellent, but I guess that's a matter of taste. The flesh is fine grained and white, but tastes muddy to me. Capt. Chet Jennings smoked part of the last cobia I caught, and it was good. But I have

144

blackened, grilled and deep-fried it with less than spectacular results.

Cobia will linger on the Southshore flats of Tampa Bay into early summer. Then they move out into deeper water to hang on buoys and range markers for easy meals of threadfin herring, scaled sardines and pinfish.

Flyfishing for Cobia

One of the harbingers of spring in West Central Florida is the arrival of cobia on the flats. While snook and redfish are getting most of the attention, cobia present the best chance for sight fishing with a fly in clear water of late winter and early spring. The big ling offer a great opportunity to hook and play an outsized fish in very shallow water on a fly.

Fly tackle for cobia should be on the order of tarpon tackle, an 8/9 weight is going to be light in some cases, while a 12 weight is hardly overkill — a 10 weight rod with a heavy duty saltwater reel with 200 yards of 30 pound backing will handle most cobia. Saltwater tapered floating lines are the best choice when sight casting to ling. Leaders should be heavy, I tie mine with a 36 inch 40# butt, followed by 30 inches of 30#, 24 inches of 25#, 18 inches of 20#, and a 24 inch shock tippet of 60#. Cobia can be just as powerful as tarpon; every knot needs to be perfect.

Fish the Flats

Chapter 14

Cobia is an excellent fish to target for beginning fly casters because this fish is not easily spooked. In fact, cobia can be downright curious. They will sometimes come right up to the boat and swim circles around it. I once hit one in the head with a jig on spinning tackle, and it took a different lure on the next cast. A shy fish the cobia is not.

As water temperatures on Tampa Bay begin to rise into the 70's in March and April, cobia will start moving onto the flats. On a calm day in clear water, I have spotted them a hundred yards from the boat, which makes a good approach to fly casting distance with a push pole or trolling motor fairly routine. These fish will often trail behind big stingrays or spotted eagle rays – check every big ray you spot, because sometimes the cobia can be underneath the ray and hard to see. Those windless days are a rarity, however. More often than not, this time of year you hunt cobia in a breezy chop, where you will appreciate the casting attributes of a heavy, weight forward flyline. Even in the chop, you can still spot fish if the water is clear.

Cobia can sometimes be maddeningly picky about what they will put in their mouths. Large patterns that mimic eels seem to attract the most attention. More important than color or pattern type is speed of retrieve. When you have a cobia interested in the fly, you have to make it believe

146

it's getting away. I don't think you can strip a fly too fast, but do not make the mistake of trying to sweep the fly along with the rod tip. Cobia are hard mouthed. To bury the hook where it won't come out requires a solid strip set with the rod tip pointed at the fish. Then bang it with a sharp jerk of the jerk of the rod once you feel the weight of the fish. Now relentless pressure is required to keep it on the line. Slack line often means a lost fish. A large arbor fly reel with lots of backing is appropriate.

I have seen cobia cruising the Southshore flats of Tampa Bay into July, but March, April, May, October and November are best months.

Fish the Flats

Running the Marks

As water temperatures rise into the 80's, cobia begin to move off the flats. They head for the deeper waters of the shipping lanes where they tend to hang around structure such as range markers and buoys.

A cloudless day with light wind is again the perfect scenario for running the marks to hunt cobia. Sometimes they can be seen right on the surface swimming counterclockwise circles around the structure. Tower boats have the edge here, but you can also spot them from deck level

Fish the Flats

on calm days with clear water – sometimes you can see them waking in orbit around the cans.

The farther away from the structure you can spot the fish, the better off you are. When I spot a cobia circling a mark, I like to get into position for comfortable casting distance. Get too close to the mark, and even if you do hook up, you have less chance of quickly pulling the fish away from the structure. If that doesn't happen soon after the hook up, a break off is the likely result.

Casting accuracy is important here as it is in shallow water. I like to let the fish circle to the back side of the mark, and then place my cast so that the fish has to come off the mark to strike. Keeping the boat a reasonable distance from the mark also lets the fish chase the bait for a few yards as they are sometimes wont to do, without spooking it by sighting the boat.

This is usually a two man operation, one angler making the cast while the other runs the boat. Soon as the fish takes, the idea is to drop the motor into reverse to help pull the fish away from the mark.

Heavy spinning tackle, saltwater baitcasting tackle, or 50 pound conventional rigs on stiff rods are appropriate for fish that can go 40 pounds and up.

I prefer artificials here because they cast inherently better than live baits. Cobia circling

149

Fish the Flats

a mark on the surface in the middle of the day are usually in a feeding mode, and in my estimation it's more important to put the bait in the cobia's face than it is to have a live bait on the hook. They are gregarious feeders and will usually try to eat anything that passes through the strike zone.

I have had particularly good luck with soft plastic shad tails, and plastic eels rigged on RipTide jig heads, which are equipped with very strong hooks.

The other advantage of artificials is that they will cover more water than is possible with live bait. I like to probe all the marks with a jig, working the water column from top to bottom. They are not always on top. This also creates a chance to hook up with other species that like to hang on the structure, such as tripletail, jacl crevalle, Spanish mackerel and sharks. If cut offs begin to occur, I add six inches of heavy wire, which doesn't seem to bother the cobia.

Running the marks is well suited to the days when it's too hot to do anything on the flats. I spend 10 minutes on each mark and then put the boat on plane to run to the next, which is like turning on the air.

150

Fish the Flats

Chapter 15

The Silver King

Tarpon are game fish in a class all by themselves. There is nothing on the flats quite like a tarpon. Not only are they much bigger than most other fish, they also get more air than Michael Jordan ever thought of.

Tarpon fishing is often a visual thing. They are primitive fish and they have an auxiliary breathing apparatus in the form of an air bladder. They sometimes come to the surface and take a gulp of air, and when they do, their silvery bodies flash like a mirror. Other times they will lay motionless on the surface, and sometimes

151

Fish the Flats

a pod of fish will swim in circles, which is called daisy chaining. Another behavior they exhibit on the surface is porpoising across the top of the water, called "greyhounding" -- these fish are seldom interested in eating.

It's interesting that one of the most effective artificials for tarpon is a fly. Why a huge fish would bother expending any energy whatsoever to catch such miniscule prey is one of the many mysteries of tarpon fishing, but so it is. However, fly-fishing for tarpon is a topic requiring a book of its own.

There are tarpon in Tampa Bay year 'round. During the winter months, many fish hole up in the headwaters of the Little Manatee River, and others hang in the hot water outflow of the power plants. Sometimes you can count more than 50 big tarpon laying on the surface at the manatee viewing center in Apollo Beach during the winter months. These fish come out onto the flats at night to feed. But early spring through late summer is the prime time to fish for tarpon on Tampa Bay.

My favorite method of tarpon fishing is to sight cast to rolling fish. This is most productive during spring and summer. Happy hour for this fishing is first light through early morning on a calm day. If there is wind and chop, the fish tend to stay down.

Tarpon laid up on the surface will gener-

152

ally strike. I like to throw four-inch shad tails on RipTide jig heads to top water fish. I use extra heavy spinning tackle with 24-pound test line, as most of the tarpon where I fish are less than 75 pounds. For bigger fish, I employ solid glass rods, extra large spinning reels, and 50-pound microfilament line. Such equipment is best suited to live bait or cut bait – it's simply too heavy to make repeated casts. With natural baits, most tarpon fishermen employ large, extra strong, extra sharp circle hooks 5/0 to 8/0. Tarpon have sandpaper lips, so a 60 to 100 pound monofilament leader is necessary if you want to bring the fish to the boat.

Rather than target tarpon, I fish for them as conditions allow. If I am on the water at daybreak and it's dead flat calm, I will spend some time looking for tarpon in May, June, July, and August. I also have a few spots where I fish for snook with surface plugs that tarpon also frequent regularly where tarpon are an incidental chance. Any plug intended for tarpon fishing should be rigged with the strongest, sharpest treble hooks available.

There are several ways to target tarpon. Capt. Billy Nobles likes to anchor around structure at the mouth of Tampa Bay, chumming with chunks of fresh caught threadfin herring while free lining big threads on a slow moving tide. He uses heavy spinning tackle with hundred pound

Fish the Flats

leaders and large circle hooks.

Captain Chet Jennings and Captain Nick Winger fish for tarpon in the upper reaches of the bay, anchoring on the deep edge of the flats around submerged rock piles. They prefer to chum with live threads or pilchards. Jennings fishes live baits for tarpon, while Winger likes one bait free-lined, and the other dead on the bottom. Tarpon are scavengers, and I have caught as many on chunks of ladyfish as I have on lures.

Capt. Matt Larsen fishes the pilings of the Gandy Bridge for tarpon, casting DOA Baitbusters to the shadow line along the pilings. He uses a trolling motor to maintain position away from the bridge, and routinely finds tarpon on the same pilings year after year.

Big fish and big tackle call for specialized knots. I rely mostly on the uni knot, but for connecting the hundred pound monofilament leader to 50# Tuff Line, I tie the Albright. It's a simple knot to learn, and well suited to connecting lines of greatly different diameters.

When casting to fish you can see on the surface, as with all fish in shallow water, accurate casting is a must. These big fish are efficient, and will not chase baits they deem to be out of range. Again, the three-foot strike zone is about right. As with cobia, I like to cast beyond the fish, and then reel the lure in front of them.

Fish the Flats

Tarpon are one of the few fish that require the lip-ripping hook set TV bass fishermen are so fond of.

Once hooked, tarpon usually take to the air. They put a whole new twist on jumping. For me, the ideal tarpon are those 60 pounds and under. They tend to jump more, and they wear out quickly. The big fish tend to drag the fight out to the point of tedium.

Tarpon are not edible, so there is really no point in killing one. However, you may kill a tarpon in Florida, if you buy a tarpon tag, which costs $50. Fiberglass mounts require only a photograph of the fish, and they age much better than skin mounts. That said, tarpon are not especially hearty and should be handled with great care. Dragging such a big fish into the boat is probably a death sentence, whether the fish swims away or not. So is the practice of removing scales. There is no point in catch and release if the fish isn't going to survive.

Seeing tarpon does not necessarily mean catching them. They can be finicky in the extreme, and sometimes they simply do not eat. Sitting in the middle of a big pod of rolling fish that will not eat is one of the most frustrating experiences in angling, much like throwing a dry fly to Atlantic salmon that are just not interested. However, it only takes a single tarpon to make up for a thousand casts.

155

Fish the Flats

Chapter 15

Playing a hooked tarpon requires relentless pressure on the part of the angler. You must fight the fish at every turn, pulling opposite to every change in direction. When the fish jumps, lower the rod tip and bend at the waist. This is called "bowing to the king", and it's designed to keep the fish from falling on a tight line and breaking you off.

When fishing live or cut bait for tarpon while anchored, make sure to have a release buoy attached to the end of the anchor line to be prepared for a chase. No matter how much line you might have on your reel, you will probably have to run the fish down.

Unlike cobia, tarpon are very skittish around outboards. Running your engine near a pod of tarpon on the surface is likely to put them down, and turn them off. Even a trolling motor is apt to spook fish. Most tarpon specialists who sight fish in shallow water are adept at poling, which is far and away the stealthiest method of closing to within casting range of tarpon.

156

Fish the Flats

Chapter 15

Jack Crevalle and Ladyfish

If jack crevalle were as tasty as they are tenacious, the population would be decimated in no time. If there is a stronger, or more aggresive fish on the local flats, I have yet to put a hook in one. But since they don't jump or taste as good as some of the more glamorous species, there is a stigma about catching jacks, and some anglers rank jacks right down there with saltwater cat-fish.

So it is that jack crevalle are not a target species for most flats fishermen. Nevertheless,

157

Fish the Flats

few anglers would pass up a chance to throw a lure into a pod of frenzied jacks. Pound for pound, no fish match them for power or endurance, and they are usually willing. When they get up around 10 or 15 pounds, a couple of fish can turn arms and wrists to jelly.

The surest way to draw a strike from a jack is to try and take the lure away. If the fish wants it, there is no way you can reel it fast enough. I like to throw big surface plugs at jacks The method is to make a long cast, point the rod tip at the surface and reel like mad. When a plug skips across the surface making noise, more in the air than it is in the water, the speed is about right. Zara Spooks, Top Dogs, and other surface plugs will all draw vicious strikes when the jacks are in the mood. But when they are really boiling the water, it doesn't much matter what you pitch into the melee.

Some anglers tell me they do not like catching jacks, and that's hard to fathom. Here's a fish that outpulls anything you're apt to set a hook into. I don't need to catch a dozen of them, mind you, but a couple is always a good thing. Jack crevalle is one of the roughest cusomers encounterd on the the flats, and I will never pass one up. Food quality is said to be poor, but I can't say for sure, because I've never eaten one. But guess what? Tarpon aren't edible, either. But because they jump a little, they're so big and they are harder to catch, they get more glory. Even so, some of the more archaic local anglers will not seek to bend a rod with anything they can't eat. That's a truly bizarre attitude if you ask me. If somebody needs to eat fish that bad, he'd be better off selling his boat and his tackle and buy his fish at market. He sure shouldn't waste his money on this book. Store bought fish are much cheaper, and a sure thing, whereas fishing with a hook and line is fraught with uncertainty

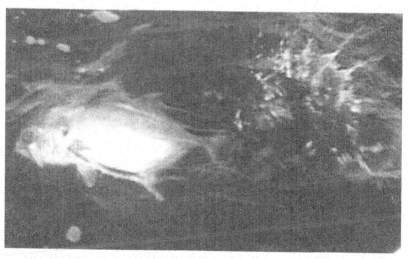

To trigger explosive strikes from jacks on surface plugs, point the rod tip at the water and reel the plug at warp speed and hang on!

159

Fish the Flats

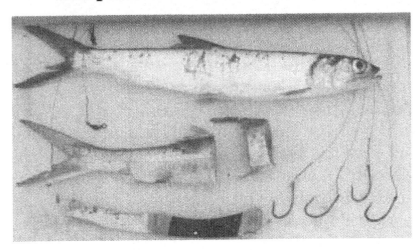

Ladyfish

Ladyfish are another species that fight way out of proportion to size, which is not surprising, as they are related to tarpon. They average a couple of pounds, take drag, and jump like crazy. They also make good bait for big snook, tarpon, and sharks. Ladyfish are ideally suited to children. They travel in schools, and are usually willing to hit a jig almost as readily as they will a live shrimp or pilchard. You find them in the same channels you find jacks; they just make a slightly smaller disturbance on the surface. Birds will follow either fish when they are ravaging bait.

Both ladyfish and jacks are ideal targets for novice saltwater fly fishermen. Ladyfish have a harder time throwing a fly than they do a jig head, but their very abrasive lips are murder on

Fish the Flats

flies. If I am targeting ladyfish with a fly rod, I will use streamers tied with synthetic hair. They will strip bucktail off a fly in a heartbeat, and only one or two fish will leave you with a bare hook and a badly frayed leader. Both fish offer good practice for strip setting hooks, and playing fish on a fly rod. Big jacks will teach you everything you need to know about line control and knot tying, because they stress tackle to the limits.

Ladyfish are here year 'round and they haunt the same waters that jacks do. Big jacks will prey on them, and that's an incredible sight. A few years back in December, a school of 15 pound jacks had a pod of ladyfish bottled up in a little pool on the inside of a sandbar in the Little Manatee River. The jacks would come through the pool every 15 minutes or so with a great commotion, leaving chunks of ladyfish behind them as they circled out to deeper water. Three of us caught them til our arm muscles turned to mush.

Both fish are ideal targets for beginning saltwater fly fishermen because they are so aggressive. You don't need a delicate presentation, nor do you need to cast far. Just keep the fly moving with long, fast strips. A seven weight rod is perfect for ladyfish, but big jacks will hurt you with anything less than a nine weight.

161

Fish the Flats

Chapter 16

Frenzied sea birds are working over a school of baitfish on the surface, while jacks or ladyfish bring it on from below. In water deeper than six feet the predators could be Spanish mackerel. Jacks will make a big disturbance on the surface with lots of noise. Ladyfish strikes are less dramatic. Spanish mackerel will occasionally launch high into the air.

162

Fish the Flats

Chapter 17

Sharks

One of my favorite winter targets is the blacktip shark. This shark is a great game fish in it's own right. It does everything a trophy snook does, and they are much more common in the three foot range. The five footers are rare on the Southshore of Tampa Bay, but I have seen a few caught in the hot water outflow of the power plant in Apollo Beach.

Blacktips are in the bay year 'round, but my best days fishing for 3 foot blacktips have come during the winter months around power plants. I have also had some incredible shark fishing in the spring, but those fish were smaller

Fish the Flats

schoolies.

Snook tackle is the right choice for these rambunctious sharks, using wire leaders and large (3/0 or bigger), chemically sharpened circle hooks. Sharks relish live pinfish, finger mullet, and ladyfish. My best day on big sharks came on frozen chunked ladyfish. They will also eat frozen squid, and frozen sardines, but if I can catch ladyfish, the fresh cut bait seems to attract more fish. I have also caught sharks on fresh chunks of catfish.

If sharks are present in great numbers, expect to get cut off frequently. I used to wonder how they were getting above the leader once they were hooked. The mystery was solved one day when a client hooked a blacktip in clear water. As the line zipped through the water, a second shark hit the line ten feet above the leader. Now I bring plenty of hooks pre rigged with a six inch length of wire.

Frozen chum blocks are effective at bringing them in, and if they are available – chumming with live pilchards is as effective on sharks as it is on snook and redfish.

Blacktips will also hit an artificial, but the cast has to be precise. I don't think they see well. Jigs have hooked most of the sharks I ever caught with lures, and I think that has mostly to do with the inherent casting accuracy of the lead head.

I also target bonnetheads during the win-

164

Fish the Flats

ter months because they are so plentiful on the Southshore Tampa Bay Flats. I have never had a bonnethead hit an artificial, and sometimes I have even had trouble hooking them with live bait. Oddly enough, the most effective bonnethead bait is frozen squid. For these fish I use my eight and a half foot flats rods with eight pound test. Wire leaders aren't necessary with circle hooks or Khale hooks, instead I use 30 pound fluorocarbon, because Bonnetheads seem to be leader shy.

Capt. Chaz Waltz with a typical bonnethead. Primarily bottom feeders, they eat crabs and shrimp and squid. A good winter target on Tampa Bay and very sporty on light tackle.

Fish the Flats

We got lucky on this blacktip, hooked while fishing for tarpon. The circle hook landed precisely where it's supposed to in the corner of the mouth, keeping those razor sharp teeth off the 80 pound monofilament leader. Only when I struck the fish with the gaff was it able to cut it off. Blacktips are fine table fare when bled, gutted, and put quickly on ice.

Fish the Flats

Flounder and Sheepshead

Flounder are difficult to target on Tampa Bay because they are widely spread out over sandy pot holes, but they are always a welcome addition as incidental catch. Most of the flounder I have ever caught hit artificials while targeting snook and redfish. They are incredibly aggressive, and their bite is much larger than the flat shape of the fish would seem to suggest. I have caught many 10 inch flounder on six inch jerk baits, so shy they are not. Flounder are not temperature sensitive, and they are caught all year long in Florida.

The limit is 12 inches, but the flounder I've

caught over the past 10 years on Tampa Bay average 15 inches, with my biggest flounder a hefty 22 incher. The reason flounder are prized is because they are as tasty a fish as salt water has to offer.

The best live bait for flounder is probably chubs, at least that's what the local experts tout, and that makes sense; you find chubs in shallow water over sandy bottom, which is also where you find flounder. But shrimp, sardines and squid will also catch them.

The best artificial bait is a small jig hopped slowly through sandy potholes or on the edge of the grass line where it meets the sand. I spot a lot of flounder while poling for redfish. These fish have proved to be uncatchable once spooked, but if I see a few flounder in a particular spot, I will approach it with caution on another day, probing well ahead of the boat, making long casts with a small jig.

Sheepshead

The reason I lumped flounder and sheepshead together in this chapter is because their table qualities are both excellent. Sheepshead are much easier to target than flounder. They are more plentiful, they hang on barnacle encrusted structure, and they respond to chum. Most anglers on Tampa Bay target them during the winter months.

The most productive method of catching sheepshead is to scrape barnacles off pilings with a hoe or shovel, then bait a long shanked #1 hook with a bit of shrimp. It's said you have to set the hook just ahead of the bite to catch sheepshead – a tribute to the fish's ability to peck the bait off the hook before you know you had a hit. This type of fishing is perfectly suited to low stretch, highly sensitive microfilament line such as Power Pro or Tuff Line. Sheepshead also require a stiff rod with plenty of muscle. They are stubby and powerful, and will take you back into structure quickly as any snook.

Sheepshead are among the tastiest of fish, and the head and bones also make excellent fish stock for use in soups or chowders. They are a bugger to fillet, however. Their scales are kin to armor plate, and their fins are tipped with needle sharp spines. Even with a cutting glove and a sharp knife, I usually wind up pricking myself once or twice with every batch of sheepshead I clean. But the resulting filets are well worth the effort.

I have only caught one sheepshead ever on an artificial (it hit a jig around a bridge piling), though I have seen several follow lures on the winter flats. And if you think redfish and snook are spooky in shallow water, sheepshead are outright paranoid. Poling to within casting dis-

169

Fish the Flats

tance without spooking them is a practical impossibility.

They are easier to catch in deeper water, but they are still very adept at pecking a bait off a hook. One look at their cartoon character teeth will explain how they can bite soft wire hooks in two. They do, after all, chew barnacles for a living. There is nothing easy about fishing for sheepshead, but once the technique of the quick hook set on the first tap is mastered, the fish will start coming to the net.

Striped, toothy, and prickly -- sheepshead are worth the effort to catch and clean. Few fish in Florida eat better.

Fish the Flats

Chapter 19

Targets of Opportunity

One of the great things about fishing on Tampa Bay is the variety of saltwater angling opportunity it affords. For example on a fly fishing outing with Capt. Art Paiva, we waded the flats for a few hours one Sunday morning with only a single swirl to show for our efforts. Despite a perfectly windless morning with a strong falling tide, we couldn't buy a fish. So after a

171

Fish the Flats

couple of hours of flailing the water to a froth with flylines, we opted to return to the boat to net some of the plentiful bait we were seeing as we waded. The grass flat was covered by a huge school of greenbacks. With a few throws of the net, we were able to put some greenies in the well . Then we headed north to check out some other spots for tarpon.

Enroute we encountered a massive school of threadfin herring, which are handy as tarpon baits. A single throw of a large mesh 10 foot net by Capt. Paiva caught more bait than we could use in a week, so we released most of it, kept a few dozen for the livewell, and went on our way.

We were cruising along the shoreline near a power plant inlet when I spotted some rolling tarpon. It was about 10 o'clock in the morning and still dead calm – the water clear. I quickly unlimbered my 12-weight fly rod and got into position on the bow of the boat. As we motored toward the tarpon, I heard Capt. Paiva shout cobia, and sure enough there were three shadows making their way across the sand in very shallow water less than half the distacnce to the tarpon. I was unable to get a cast off right away, but after some maneuvering Capt. Paiva positioned the boat perfectly, and I laid the fluorescent orange flyline right across the noses of the three cobia. My cast was about 10 feet too long, and the three cobia spooked, and the tar-

172

Fish the Flats

pon disappeared.

We turned the boat around to look for them, and a moment later spotted a single shadow heading up the beach -- another cobia. Again Capt. Paiva got me into range, and this time I made a good cast. The big fish turned on the fly but missed it. Capt. Art was ready with live bait however and cast it well beyond the fish. When the cobia came near the bait, the threadfin sped away. Another well placed cast put the bait in front of the big cobia again. This time it circled the bait – a sure sign of intention to dine. A moment later the fish put the bait in its mouth and Capt. Paiva set the hook. Only then did I realize how big the fish really was as it surged through the calm water like a miniature submarine in high gear.

I took pictures while Capt. Paiva fought the fish on 10 pound test line. It was apparently well hooked, but the 30-pound leader was wrapped around the cobia's head. It was a cause of concern throughout much of the battle, and it finally came free with a frightening ping, but did'n break. About 30 minutes later the big fish finally came to the side of the boat, where I gaffed it, brought it aboard, and got out of the way as more than fifty pounds of solid muscle began to thrash around. A few minutes later the cobia finally wore it out, and coughed up a stingray the size of dinner plate, leaving it's barbed tail protruding

173

Fish the Flats

through one side of the big cobia's jaw. The old fish showed plenty of battle scars. Part of his tail had been chewed off at one time, and a long scar along the dorsal fin appeared to have made by an attempt with a gaff or spear gun.

Cobia are often hooked this way because the have little fear of man, boat or beast. But hooking such fish and landing them is two different things. Your tackle has to be up to snuff or you will be in for a long fight at best, or a quick break off in the worst case scenario. I have since learned to carry at least one rod on the boat at all times that gives you a shot at such targets of opportunity.

The line on this rod should be fresh and stout enough to handle a big fish on open water. Ten-pound test is pretty minimal, and even 20-pound test would make for a long day on big tarpon, but I like to rig my big fish rod for the 50-pound fish because they are more common than the hundred pounders. I also rig a heavy leader; say 60-pound test, and make sure that the hook is up to the task. Some of the new microfilament lines are well suited to this work because of their fine diameter for great strength, their resistance to abrasion, and their casting properties.

By having a heavy duty rod on hand, when a target of opportunity wakes your way, you can give it your best shot.

Currently, I carry an extra heavy 71/2 foot

174

Fish the Flats

spinning rod, rigged with 24 pound test monofilament, a 3 foot 60 pound leader, and a stout Rip Tide half ounce jig head and a four inch shad tail. Any fish under 100 pounds is fair game for this outfit.

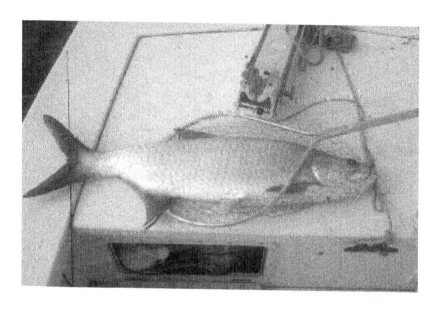

Rolling tarpon and waking cobia are the two most prevalent opportunities to tange with very big fish in shallow water on the Tampa Bay Flats A heavy spinning rod rigged with a 1/2 ounce RipTide jig head anda four inch shad tail is a proven rig for cobia, tarpon, bull reds, and trophy snook.

Fish the Flats

John Oliverio battles a cobia on a light rod. The fish happened to pass by while we were stalking red fish.

Fish the Flats

Chapter 20

Tackle Up for Spanish Mackerel

Since the inshore net ban was passed in Florida more than five years ago, Spanish mackerel have made an incredible comeback in the waters of West Central Florida. There are Spanish mackerel in Tampa Bay all year long, but it is in early spring, summer and fall when the big schools ravage baitfish up and down the bay. The catching part can be easy when the macks are slashing through bait that's balled up on the surface, but a little forethought will go a long way in perfecting an approach to mackerel fishing.

177

Fish the Flats

Spanish mackerel are toothy, and will cut off hooks and lures unless your leader is up to snuff. Wire leaders may prevent tackle losses, but mackerel specialists claim wire leaders deter strikes.

Finding mackerel on Tampa Bay is seldom a problem spring, summer and fall. They will hang close to the schools of bait around the ship channels, and on the range markers. When you see bait on the surface, there will generally be macks nearby. Sometimes the bait will ball up in a tight wad, and you will actually see the mackerel flying through it. Seagulls diving on schools of threadfin herring is a sure sign that the macks are feeding – the birds are picking up leftovers from the mack attack. Other times, mackerel stay deep, and may not hit artificials as readily as live bait.

Rigging for mackerel can be an exercise in frustration if it's not geared to this razor mouthed fish. Spanish mackerel have sharp teeth that can slice through 30-pound monofilament. A wire leader will prevent cut offs, but it can also deter strikes. 60-pound mono is a about right for macks, regular fishing line is fine but mackerel hit leader knots on occasion. Twenty-pound test monofilament stands up to this better than the light line used on the flats. Abrasion resistant microfilaments or braids work well, but occasional cut offs will ever be a part of mackerel fish-

178

ing.

My favorite mackerel lure is a one-ounce chrome spoon. I like it rigged with a #1 live bait hook, with the barb bent down to facilitate removal. I also fix a black or green barrel swivel to the lure with a split ring. Treble hooks are not necessary for these willing fighters. Gang trebles will necessarily slow things on a hot bite, complicating hook removal, and can do serious injury to fish you may want to release, and despite their voracity, mackerel are fragile. There is a minimum size of 12 inches in Florida.

The big advantage to the chrome spoon with a single hook is that you can fish it with live bait, or a strip of cut squid when they won't take the naked artificial. A nose hooked pilchard or threadfin herring will cast and retrieve just fine on the spoon. When rigged with natural baits, I will let the spoon go all the way down to the bottom; this method covers the entire water column. The speed of the retrieve with bait on the lure should be much slower than with bare metal. Soon as something edible is attached to the spoon, it seems to be more productive when you give the fish a chance to smell it. But with a bare lure, try to generate an impulse strike by taking the lure away with a fast retrieve, imitating a panicked baitfish trying to escape. On days when I run out of spoons, a three eight ounce jig head rigged with a live bait will do the trick, but it

179

Fish the Flats

won't cast as far or cover the water column as fast. The shorter overall length of the jig will also put the mack's teeth on the leader more often, which creates a greater likelihood of cutoffs.

Use a long shanked hook for mackerel when fishing real bait, – it puts more distance between the mack's teeth and the leader. On a slow bite when the only thing they'll take is cut bait drifted through a chum slick, make every fish count by keeping the mack's teeth off the leader. If the fish is allowed to swallow the bait, a cut off is likely.

Some days mackerel are particularly rambunctious and will hit everything you throw at them. The down side to this is that you go through tackle because they will bite at the line as it moves through the water. Other times, they become sullen and have to be chummed up. A cast net and a bunch of threadfin herring will usually put the mackerel in the mood, but it requires more patience, and a larger net with larger mesh than what would normally be used for pilchards in shallow water. A ten or twelve foot net with half inch mesh is about right for threadfins.

One of the great rewards of catching mackerel is that they are good to eat — in flavor, and in promoting good health. Spanish mackerel are high in the Omega 3 oil that is very good for the heart. I often hear the complaint from some anglers that mackerel are "fishy" tasting. I sus-

Fish the Flats

pect that perception is related to poor handling of the fish after they are caught.

Mackerel need to be put on ice immediately after being landed for two reasons. One is to keep the fish firm and fresh tasting, and the other is to keep them from making a bloody mess of your boat. Mackerel bleed freely, and will choke up all of the stuff they have been gorging themselves on, which is good cause to avoid treble hooks. When I get a hooked keeper ready to land, I open the cooler lid and jack the mack right into the box. The barb-less hook usually falls right out, so I can close the cooler lid and get back to fishing. Any mess the thrashing fish makes is confined to the cooler. A good rule of thumb is to kill only the fish you will eat that same day. Mackerel do not fare as well when refrigerated overnight – better to freeze what you won't eat the day of the catch. Better still to kill only what you can eat that day.

Few fish are easier to filet than Spanish mackerel. A sharp knife and a flat surface covered with newspaper make it anti skid and easy to clean. I run the knife blade down to the backbone behind the gills, then turn it parallel to the spine and slice off the filet. Turn the fish over and repeat. I remove the skin in the same manner, starting from the tail. Then I cut the filet in half, right down the center of the bloodline. I take great care to trim away all of this dark col-

181

Fish the Flats

ored flesh. After that and a good freshwater rinse, it's ready to be cooked according to your favorite fish recipe.

Spanish mackerel are wonderful game fish – very sporty on the same tackle employed in flats fishing. Speedy, strong, and willing, the mackerel fight is way out of proportion to the size of the fish. And to top it off they are plentiful, accessible to near shore anglers, good to eat, and good for you.

Jacking mackerel into an iced cooler makes for the best possible table quality, and minimizes the mess on the boat.

Fish the Flats

Visit Captain Fred's Website:

Tampabayfishingguide.com

Other books by the Captain available on the website:

Catch Snook!

A Bar Player's Guide to Winning Darts

Also available:

Bad to the Bone! 8 1/2 foot light tackle Flats Rods -- Hand crafted and designed by Capt. Fred.

Contact the Captain:

Capt. Fred Everson
1807 Kofresi Ct.
Ruskin, FL 33570

(813) 641-7697

email: lhuntsnook@aol.com

Fish the Flats

CPSIA information can be obtained
at www.ICGtesting.com
Printed in the USA
BVOW08s0835201217
503308BV00001B/396/P